P9-DEJ-357

THE ILLUSTRATED

Compendium =OF=

UGLY

ENGLISH

Words

THE ILLUSTRATED Compendium :OF: UGLY ENGLISH Words

Including Phlegm, Chunky, Moist, and More

Tyler Vendetti
Illustrated by Rebecca Pry

For Cody Vendetti.
(See? I told you I'd make you famous.)

The Illustrated Compendium of Ugly English Words

Copyright © 2019 by Whalen Book Works LLC.

This is an officially licensed book by Whalen Book Works LLC.

All rights reserved under the Pan-American and International Copyright Conventions. No part of this book may be reproduced in whole or in part, scanned, photocopied, recorded, distributed in any printed or electronic form, or reproduced in any matter whatsoever, or by any information storage and retrieval system known or hereafter invented, without express written permission of the publisher except in the case of brief quotations embodied in critical articles and reviews.

The scanning, uploading, and distribution of this book via the Internet or via any other means without permission of the publisher is illegal and punishable by law. Please support author's rights, and do not participate in or encourage piracy of copyrighted materials.

13-digit ISBN: 978-1-732-51263-4
10-digit ISBN: 1-732-51263-9

This book may be ordered by mail from the publisher. Please include $5.99 for postage and handling. Please support your local bookseller first!

Books published by Whalen Book Works are available at special discounts when purchased in bulk. For more information, please email us at info@whalenbookworks.com.

Whalen Book Works
68 North Street
Kennebunkport, ME 04046

www.whalenbookworks.com

Cover and interior design by Melissa Gerber
Typography: Times New Roman, Adobe Caslon, ITC Caslon 224, Minya Nouvelle Italic, Times LT STD, and Times.
Printed in China
3 4 5 6 7 8 9 0

INTRODUCTION

I was sixteen when I first learned what *astronaut* meant. It was 2009, the fall of my junior year of high school, and in retaliation against my mother, who had spent the previous decade ushering me from one Spanish class to the next against my will, I signed up for a new foreign language, one that I knew would send her head rolling across the floor.

"Latin?!" she screeched. "You can't even *use* Latin! It's a dead language! Why would you want to learn a dead language?!" Well, my reasons were threefold. First, the thought of sitting through another Spanish lesson filled with *eñes* and upside-down punctuation marks while my mother stood by wringing her hands in delight made my stomach churn. Second, because Latin is, in fact, a dead language that is no longer spoken aloud, there was a near guarantee that I would never have to take an oral exam ever again, a prospect too promising to ignore. And third, I simply wanted to. Since the age of three, I had been an unabashed bookworm, reading and writing and ingesting as much content as my little walnut brain could hold. The English language fascinated me and I wanted to learn everything about it that I could, to immerse myself in the world of words.

It was not until the first day of class, though, after everyone had settled into their seats and thrown the obligatory pencils into the ceiling, that I realized just how deep this passion ran. The teacher, an unseasonably jolly woman, shuffled in, her eyes glistening with pride at the sight of an overflowing classroom. As the chatter began to die down, she turned to the whiteboard, popped open a marker, and wrote, in big block letters: ASTRONAUT.

"What does this mean?" she said, pointing to the word as if it were a hieroglyphic we had never seen before.

"Someone who goes out into space!" one student shouted, already eager to prove himself.

"Yes, but what does it *really* mean?" A dozen faces blinked before her, suddenly questioning their knowledge of basic space terminology. With a knowing smile, she split the word in two, scribbling *astro-* and *-naut* on separate ends of the board. She began to explain the etymology of each: *astro-* comes from the Latin word *astrum* meaning "star," while *-naut* comes from the Greek word *nautes* meaning "sailor." When combined and translated, then, the word astronaut means "star sailor."

It was in that moment, when I realized the hidden beauty behind this everyday word, that my love for language truly ignited, growing from a glimmer into a full-blown blaze. I continued to take Latin throughout high school and into college, where I proudly declared my English major and began writing about words for any and all outlets that would let me. Cute words. Kooky words. Dirty words. Medical words. Words so long and convoluted, they almost looked fake. None were safe from my all-consuming fascination.

But out of all the words that I studied, there was one type of word that I kept returning to, one category that captivated me more than all the rest: ugly words. I became enamored by ugly words for the same reason that most people are drawn to beautiful ones: they're universal. While there are certain words that everyone collectively loves (*labyrinthine, somnambulist, serendipity, imbroglio*), there are also

words that everyone collectively hates (*moist*, *phlegm*, *lugubrious*, *curd*). But why? What makes *yolk* more repulsive than *ripple* or *epiphany* more pleasing than *ooze*? How does one combination of letters cause some people to cringe and another, to swoon? Why do some words send shivers down our spines while others release butterflies in our hearts?

In writing this book, I intended to find out.

And for the most part, I did. In amassing this collection of the English language's ugliest words, I learned that a word's repulsiveness comes down to one of three things.

So, what makes a word turn-your-stomach ugly?

- **The nature of the word's meaning.** Many of the terms in this dictionary—*barf*, *maggot*, *scab*—describe items that are, in real life, gross. Conversely, words that most of us consider beautiful—*felicity*, *ebullience*, *bubble*—represent concepts or objects that are positive or refreshing.

- **The pre-existing association the reader or speaker has with the word.** Take *moist*, for example. While there is nothing gross about the physical structure or sound of the word itself—compared to, say, *grotesque*, which requires a series of grunts just to say it aloud—most people have a bad association with it because they've heard it been used in a negative context. Maybe someone mockingly referred to them as *moist* at some point in their lives. Maybe they have had an uncomfortable experience during which the word was mentioned. Maybe they've encountered an annoying coworker who loves the word so much, they've made it their mission to use it as much as possible, causing everyone in the office to automatically hate it. No matter the reason, the association stuck, exiling the term to language limbo for the rest of time.

- **The sound or look of the word.** Judging a term's beauty (or lack thereof) by its appearance or tone, rather than its meaning, is a common practice known as phonaesthetics. It's the method that brought us "cellar door," a phrase so widely considered beautiful that it's become the subject of books, bands, and creepy sci-fi movies featuring Jake Gyllenhaal and bunnies. According to phonaesthetics, words with multiple syllables that contain smooth letters like *l*, *r*, and *m* are more likely to be considered beautiful than single-syllable words containing strong letters like *f* or *k*. Certain letter combinations, especially those that force you to reach deep into your throat (like *unk*) or unwittingly spit on your friends (like *th*) also detract from a word's beauty.

These were the most common answers I found to the question "what makes a word gross or ugly," and I did my darndest to incorporate as many examples of each that I could. There were, however, a few instances where I felt the need to omit certain terms, despite how well they may have fit into these categories. I'm talking about the hate speech, the slurs, the attacks on body image, and the insults intended to convince those who are considered different that they are lesser or unworthy. Those will not be included in this book, and anyone who has come here looking for them may seek them elsewhere, like the inside of a bathroom stall or the comments thread of any popular internet article.

That's not what this book is about. This book is about the words that make us squirm, the words that induce nervous giggle fits, and the words that unite us all in our hatred of them. It will make you cringe, it will (hopefully) make you laugh, and if I'm lucky, it will teach you something new and reveal the hidden beauty behind the words you hear every day. And who knows? Maybe it will even convince you to take a Latin class or two.

How to Use This Book

First, grip the edges of the book firmly in both hands. Look at the cover, the introduction, the heartwarming entries. Flip through the illustrations, the detailed etymologies, the offensively bad puns, the vivid and slightly unsettling descriptions. Are you intrigued? Does it seem appealing? Funny? Informative, even? Would you display this book on a coffee table before the dinner guests arrive? Read it to the children before bed? Stuff it in Grandma's stocking on Christmas Eve in an attempt to get her to read more?

If the answer is "No," then you have my permission return this book to the shelf. Not because I'm bitter or closed-minded or upset that you won't let me indoctrinate your children, but because this compendium covers a very specific topic—the study of language—and I am fully aware that it may not be everyone's cup of tea. I'm not looking to put words in your mouth or in your library, so if you're not a fan of the aforementioned subjects, feel free to turn back now. I won't hold it against you.

If you are, however, a bona fide word nerd and you are ready to embark on this journey, here are a few tips to help you out along the way.

- As you read, you will notice that the entries in this book are arranged alphabetically rather than by their degree of ugliness. There are two reasons for that: one, because ugliness is hard to quantify and two, because when your Aunt Patti inevitably asks, "Is *moist* in there?" we want her to be able to find it with ease. We did this for you, Auntie P.

- All entries include a pronunciation guide, an etymology blurb, and a list of common meanings organized from least to most funny, as determined by the author. Some also include detailed illustrations to emphasize their degree of gross. If effective, they will induce vomiting or at the very least, discomfort. Apologies in advance.

- Cross-references are indicated by **bold italics** and may appear at the beginning, middle, or end of a definition, or behind the couch where they've been hiding the whole time. (Italics are also used throughout this book to signify a publication or media title and to emphasize all of the sarcastic comments.)

- Some entries also feature quotes. These are primarily employed to clarify a word's meaning, garner a laugh, or bolster the argument that it is ugly or gross in some capacity. If it accomplishes none of those things, that's fine. This is just to let you know that we tried.

Now, those are all the ways that you can use this book on a small scale. On a larger scale, this book can be used to enrich your vocabulary, stimulate the senses, or inspire a Twitter movement to ban any and all repulsive terms from the English language (#DownWithDictionaries). More than anything, though, this compendium can be used as a reminder that, despite all of our differences (physically, politically, romantically), deep down, we all share the same hopes, the same dreams, and the same primal hatred for the terms that make us go, "Ugh, why would you even say that?!"

Pronunciation Guide

Every word in this book is accompanied by a pronunciation guide, enclosed in brackets, outlining exactly how you have been saying the word wrong your entire life. Each entry includes a slew of phonetic symbols that are meant to be helpful but will ultimately cause more confusion. In an effort to alleviate some of the befuddlement, the symbols are explained below.

Vowels

i = What's the plural of moose? **Meese?**

i = Don't get all **sappy** on me, tree.

ɪ = Crock-Pots are so **lit**.

ɛ = Well, if it isn't my old friend, Hot **Mess**.

ɛ = Girl, I'm thirty-four. I'm dating to **marry**.

æ = Adulthood! It's a **trap**!

ɑ = Luke, I am your **father**. Seriously. Here's the DNA test.

ɑ = I'm **not** being your Sugar Mama, Derek. I only make fifty cents more than you.

ɔ, ɑ = He said, "I'll be watching you like a **hawk**," then perched himself on my windowsill.

ə = Anyone up for a game of flip the House of Representatives? No? Just flip **cup** then?

ʊ = My ideal guy is Kevin Bacon from **Footloose**.

u = Wait, so does **moose** not have a plural? Should I just say meese?

ə = Not to brag, but I know all twenty-six letters of the **alphabet**.

ɔr = Save a **horse**, ride a magic carpet.

ər = McDonald's drive-thrus are a blessing and a **curse**.

ɪ(ə)r = **Here's** the thing: I don't care.

ɛ(ə)r = I double-dog **dare** you to come meese tipping with me tonight.

ʊ(ə)r = She **lured** me out of the house using a box of Thin Mints.

eɪ = **Race** you to rock-bottom!

aɪ = He was raised by **mice**-sized wolves.

aʊ = You shut your dirty **mouth**.

oʊ = Over the river and through the woods and across the **moat** and past the erupting volcano to Grandmother's house we go.

ɔɪ = Dude, you beat Oregon Trail? **Noice**.

æ̃ = Who needs friends when you have enamel **pins**?

ɑ̃ = The name's **Bond**. James Cordelia Bond.

Consonants

b = Gunshot wounds. **Betcha** can't have just one.

d = **Don't** you wish your girlfriend were financially responsible like me?

dʒ = **Joke's** on you, I don't even have a 401(k)!

ð = **That's** not what I said, Cheryl.

f = Listen, I know you're only six, but **figure** it out.

g = **Get** out of here. Go on! Get!

h = **Howdy**, partner. Glad we finally went into business together.

j = Don't be a **yes** man, be a yasssss man.

k = Are you gonna **kiss** me or not?

l = Get in, **loser**. We're going parka shopping.

m = It's like you haven't even *read* Betty White's **memoir**.

n = **Never** say "never say never."

ŋ = If you like it, then you better put a **ring** on it. No, not an onion ring.

p = Death to **pickle** chips.

r = This week on Comedy Central: the **Roast** of Tom Cruise.

s = Don't get mad, get even. Then get a house far, far away **so** no one can find you.

ʃ = I totally **ship** it.

t = When the going gets **tough**, nap.

tʃ = Ch-ch-ch-**chia**!

θ = Don't **think**. Just drink.

v = This is bad. **Very** bad. Like, "Trump for President" bad.

w = **Winter** is coming. She RSVPed and everything.

z = I don't date anyone who doesn't know what **zeitgeist** means.

ʒ = I can't hang out today. I need to finish my **vision** board.

x = Welcome to **Loch** Ness, the home of Nessie and lots of bacteria.

Lastly, the ' symbol indicates where the stress falls in each word. If, for example, the ' symbol is at the beginning of a syllable, then the primary stress is at the beginning of the word, and so on.

acrid

acrid (adjective | /ˈækrəd/): Deeply bitter; corrosive; so unpleasant in taste or odor that it causes people to retch instantaneously and shriek the word into the air like a pained battle cry: "ACKKKKK-RID."

Origin: First appearing in 1557, *acrid* was originally defined as "locust" thanks to Sir John Cheke, who incorporated this word (borrowed from the Greek *ἀκρίδ-*) into his rendition of the Greek New Testament. Its modern definition ("pungent") formed later during the 1600s from the Latin term *acer,* meaning "sharp to the senses." The irregular structure of the word acrid suggests, too, that it may have been influenced by *acrimonious*, meaning "bitter."

❝ My first impression as I opened the door was that a fire had broken out, for the room was so filled with smoke that the light of the lamp upon the table was blurred by it. As I entered, however, my fears were set at rest, for it was the acrid fumes of strong coarse tobacco which took me by the throat and set me coughing. ❞

—*John Watson,*
The Hound of the Baskervilles

accumulation (noun | /əˌkjum(j)əˈleɪʃ(ə)n/):

The gradual acquisition of something, usually rain, or, if you are a millennial, student debt and internalized shame for being a millennial. *Accumulation* is considered ugly by many for how closely the beginning of it resembles the sound of a sneeze. More like acCHU-mulation, am I right?

Origin: Partly from the Middle French *accumulacion* (meaning "heap"), partly from the Latin *accumulātiōn* (meaning "the act of piling up"), partly from the local weatherman's desperate need for more rain synonyms.

> ❝ Trying to be happy by accumulating possessions is like trying to satisfy hunger by taping sandwiches all over my body. ❞
>
> —*Roger J. Corless,* Vision of Buddhism: The Space Under the Tree

actually

(adverb | /ˈæk(t)ʃ(əw)əli/): In truth or in reality. It is the word the class know-it-all uses right before they are about to correct your small, slip-of-the-tongue mistake, and it is usually followed by a brag disguised as a claim to authority. For example: "*Actually*, the sky is an azure blue, not a periwinkle blue. I studied Color Theory in Art School, so I would know." The sudden desire to roll your eyes and duct tape the mouth of the "actually" offender in these moments is what makes this word so plainly awful.

Origin: Take the French *actual* or the Latin *actualis* and mash it with the suffix *-ly*, and you get this monstrosity.

> ❝People sometimes say that the way things happen in movies is unreal, but actually it's the way things happen in life that's unreal.❞
>
> —*Andy Warhol,* The Philosophy of Andy Warhol (From A to B and Back Again)

adulting (noun | /əˈdəltɪŋ/): The act of behaving like an

adult. Members of the older generation despise this term for being a not-so-cute way for youths to opt out of maturing by viewing it as a choice rather than an obligation. As in, "I paid rent yesterday because I am good at adulting" instead of "I paid rent yesterday because I am a twenty-nine-year-old man and if I refuse, I will be evicted." In a world where financial independence from your parents is a true accomplishment, not a guaranteed next step, it is hard to blame millennials for wanting to celebrate self-sufficiency.

Origin: A bastardization of the classic Latin word *adultus,* meaning "full-grown." Though the word *adult* was first invented in the fifteenth century, it did not gain popularity until the seventeenth century.

❝ Coffee, because adulting is hard. ❞

—A mug you will find in every young adult's cabinet

aioli
(noun | /eɪˈoʊli/): Mayonnaise seasoned with garlic. It may taste okay, but it sounds too much like a knock-off cannoli to escape this book.

aitchbone
(noun | /ˈeɪtʃ͜boʊn/): The butt bone, especially of an animal like cattle. Also, probably the sound you would make if you broke said butt bone in a tragic sitting accident.

Origin: A combination of the French words *nache* (meaning "rump") and *bone* (meaning "hard white tissue"). Over time, the *n* was dropped as a result of numerous mispronunciations, leading people to say "ache-bone," then eventually "aitchbone." Interestingly enough, *aitch* itself is a Middle English word meaning "the name of the letter H," which is why a cattle's aitchbone is often referred to as an "H-bone" now. No matter how you say it, though, one thing remains clear: the word aitchbone makes a sound that is music to nobody's ears.

> **❝** The foot bone's connected to the—ankle bone! The ankle bone's connected to the—leg bone! The leg bone's connected to the—wishbone-shaped butt-frame of a chunky, mud-crusted cow known as the aitchbone, ache-bone, or H-bone! Now shake those skeleton bones! **❞**

—*A nursery rhyme for young cattle ranchers*

amazeballs (noun | /əˈmeɪzbɑlz/): Simply amazing.

Probably invented by the same middle schooler who dreamt up *spazzy* or *biffle*. The public's opinion of this word can be perfectly encapsulated by a recent Slate article titled "Who coined *amazeballs* and why do they hate humanity?" The answer remains at large.

Origin: In 2009, popular celebrity blogger Perez Hilton used the word-that-shall-not-be-named in one of his posts. Before people had time to process how heart-wrenchingly bad the word was, Hilton took to Twitter to celebrate his contribution to the English language. Almost ten years later, everyone still hates him for it.

> ❝ Stop trying to make amazeballs happen. It's not going to happen. ❞
>
> —*Everyone*

amoeba
(noun | /əˈmiːbə/): A formless, single-celled organism. Similar to how supervillains always tend to reside in dank caves, macabre castles, or other settings that most people would deem unlivable, amoebas thrive in damp, moist environments, oozing along like a microscopic barf spittle. They are so hated by their own cell community that they have to *literally clone themselves* through a process called binary fission in order to reproduce, taking #ForeverAlone to a whole new level.

Origin: From the Greek word *ἀμοιβή*, meaning "alteration."

> 66 Men are rats. Listen to me. They're fleas on rats.
> Worse than that, they're amoebas on fleas on rats.
> I mean, they're too low for even the dogs to bite. 99
>
> —*Frenchy,* Grease

amok (verb / noun | /əˈmɒk/): A murderous frenzy or to scamper around madly (also known as, to run amok). Looks like the name of a *Star Wars* character, but, for some reason, isn't.

artery (noun | /ˈɑrdəri/): A large vessel that carries blood from the heart to the other parts of the body. You have probably heard it in the context of clogged arteries during a lecture from your mother or pediatrician after you were caught eating a third box of Hostess CupCakes. They might have even pulled out a photo of a clogged artery from some anatomy textbook in an attempt to make you associate delicious cupcakes with yellow, plaque-filled tubes. Little do they know that the whole situation backfired, because now when you hear the words artery and Hostess, all you can think about is sweet, sweet rebellion.

Origin: From the Anglo-Norman and Middle French *arterie,* meaning "windpipe." The Ancient Greeks also referred to arteries as windpipes and sometimes air ducts, believing that arteries do not contain any blood after death.

66 My left descending septal branch artery decided to close without consultation with any of my other organs. 99

—*George Carlin*

asinine (adjective | /ˈasɪnʌɪn/): An adjective, meaning "having the qualities of a jerk," that a bookish snake might use as an insult: "You are so assssssssinineeeee."

asphalt (noun | /ˈæˌsfɑlt/): A dark bituminous material used to cover roads and fry raw eggs on hot summer days for viral internet videos. Sounds a bit like a Brit blaming their buttocks for something in a panic: "I did not mean to fart! No, sir. That was my arse's fault. My asphalt!"

Origin: The word has roots in Old French (*aspaltoun*), Italian (*aspalto*), and Latin (*asphalton, asphaltum*), but it is primarily taken from the Greek *asphaltos* ("bitumen"), which, when broken down further, comes from the combination of the Greek *a* ("not") and *sphaltos* ("able to be thrown down"). This leads me to believe *asphalt* would be a good rapper alias. As in, "my name is Asphalt because you can't hold me down."

> 66 The road to success is paved with
> the hot asphalt of failure. 99
>
> —*Craig D. Lounsbrough*

astroturf (noun | /ˈæstroʊˌtɔrf/): A type of artificial grass commonly used in sports stadiums and public fields. It's known for its ability to singe the arms and legs of any brave player who decides to dive for the ball during a heated game, and for its absolutely ridiculous name, which was inspired by the Astrodome stadium in Houston, Texas, where it was first used.

avuncular (adjective | /əˈvʌŋkjʊlə/): Of or pertaining to an uncle; having the kind spirit of an uncle-figure; possessing a mighty need to give young family members noogies and ask them about their report cards.

Origin: Stems from Latin *avunculus*, meaning "maternal uncle." Strangely, the word also has a slang definition often noted in etymological studies: pawnbroker. Some claim this is because the idea of a benevolent uncle ("I will charge you zero dollars for this piece of cheese, because you are my niece!") became linked to the idea of helpful pawnbroker ("I will charge you only one dollar for this piece of cheese, because you are my customer and also, the cheese has started to grow mold!"), thus giving birth to this nickname.

66 Nowhere have I ever heard of Satan taking the form of an avuncular hippie. No doubt he could. It just seems inefficient. 99

—*Nick Harkaway*

awesomesauce (noun | /ˈɔːsəmsɑs/): Very

good. This word likely came about when some intoxicated twentysomething decided to put the word "awesome" in front of their favorite food so everyone would know how delicious it was, only to wake up the next day and realize their word concoction actually does the exact opposite by making everyone gag a little when they say it.

Origin: Back in the year 2000, Mike and Matt Chapman launched a cartoon series called *Homestar Runner* that quickly became a hit, with Strong Bad emerging as the breakout character. This red-faced robot became the first person (or, rather, nonperson) to utter this phrase.

> **❝Oh, all of you shut up! Andy, April is mad because you said 'awesomesauce' instead of 'I love you, too.' April, he loves you, so stop being a child.❞**
>
> —*Ron Swanson,*
> Parks and Recreation

AWESOME SAUCE

MAY INDUCE GAGGING

backwash (noun | /ˈbækˌwɑʃ/): A backward current; the

moving of water in a reverse direction; the liquid that flows from a person's mouth back into a bottle when they remove it from their lips. Or, rather, the spit water that a younger sibling uses to prevent you from stealing swigs of their drink.

Origin: *Back + wash.*

❝ Now, I know there are some polls out there saying [George W. Bush] has a 32 percent approval rating [...] Sir, pay no attention to the people who say the glass is half empty because 32 percent means it's two-thirds empty. There's still some liquid in that glass, is my point. But I wouldn't drink it. The last third is usually backwash. ❞

—*Stephen Colbert*

bae (noun | /beɪ/): A person's significant other. Ask someone between the ages of fifteen and twenty-one and they will tell you that bae means "before anyone else" or that it is a shortened form of babe or baby. Ask anyone twenty-one and up, and they will tell you it is the worst pet name ever invented, behind maybe "Princess" or "Sugarhoneydumpling."

Origin: No one knows, but there are some theories. The leading one points to the 2013 "bae caught me slippin'" meme that features candid shots of people sleeping, made to look like they were taken by the person's "bae" when they were actually taken by themselves. Sad? Yes. Funny? Also yes. *The New York Times* officially translated "bae caught me slippin'" into "babe caught me sleeping" in an article later that year. Which raises the question: Will we see a future where words can have more than five letters? Or will the younger generation shorten them all for convenience until we are all speaking in acronyms?

❝ Are we at the beach? Because I am on bae watch right now. ❞

—Instagram caption of a couple at the beach tagged with hashtags like #aybaebae and #funinthesun

balm (noun | /bɑ(l)m/): Ointment used to soothe the skin. When
applied to an injury (see: **wound**), it decreases pain. When spoken aloud, it
increases the chances that someone will snap at you and throw your EOS canister
down a well. Why? The "al" combination in the middle forces you to use the
back of your tongue to usher the sound out of your mouth, which is not only
uncomfortable but creates the sensation that you are about to vomit up the eggs
Benedict that you just ate for breakfast.

Origin: From the Old French word *basme* and the Latin word *balsamum*. Both terms
mean "balsam," which is the sweet-smelling oil that plants of the *Balsamodendron*
genus exude and could turn even the Sahara into a moist mud puddle.

66 There is a politeness so terrible, that rage beside it is balm. **99**

—*Minna Antrim*

barf

(verb / noun | /barf/): The act of regurgitating food (usually into a toilet or onto your best friend's lap after a night of reckless decisions); the product of said regurgitation, which is often so sour and chunky that it inspires additional barfing. The word itself sounds like the noise you make right before you project this liquid onto some poor Uber driver's back seat.

Origin: Most etymology sites cannot identify the origin of this term, calling it "probably imitative." But if that were true, this entry would look less like *barf* and more like *blerahhhhhhhhf.*

> **❝** Think about what happens on Earth when you throw up. You throw up and you have a bag of something horrible and then you throw it away. But if I have this bag, what am I going to do with it? This bag is going to stay with me in space for months, so we want a really good barf bag. **❞**
>
> —*Astronaut Chris Hadfield*

barnacle (noun | /ˈbɑːnək(ə)l/): A crustacean that attaches

itself to submerged surfaces and hardens, forming tiny bulges that look like unpopped pimples or lizard scales or some other nasty thing designed to make your skin crawl. Can also refer to the metal bar inserted between a horse's lips to restrain them, or to a type of wild goose found in arctic waters.

Origin: Though "crustacean" is the most well-known definition of this word, the goose etymology predates it by almost 200 years and poses no discernible connection to the arthropod term. Why? Unclear. Some ancient superstitions claim that arctic geese used to hatch from barnacles, an idea that developed as a result of some barnacles' feathered shells. Others believed that barnacles forming on trees near the shore would drop from their branches into the water and transform into geese. Sure, that's not exactly how birth works, but isn't it fun to imagine a group of crusty little balls morphing into geese when they touch water?

> ❝ Maybe a story will cheer you up. It's called 'The Ugly Barnacle': Once there was an ugly barnacle. He was so ugly that everyone died. The End. ❞

—*Patrick Star,* Spongebob Squarepants

bladderwort (noun | /ˈblædərwɔ(ə)rt/):

Bladderwort does not mean "a wart on your bladder" as you might think. It refers instead to a type of carnivorous plant that has sac-like, air-filled leaves used to keep it afloat in water. These floaties of the shrub world may look like elegant water stars bobbing on the surface of a pond, but do not be fooled: they are stone-cold killers.

Origin: Combination of the word *bladder* (from the Germanic term *blodram* meaning "something inflated") and *wort* (from the Old English word *wyrt* meaning "herb"). When combined, then, this word literally means "inflated herb."

> **❝** The sundew actually digests its prey with the help of a gastric juice similar to what is found in the stomach of animals; but the bladderwort and pitcher-plants can only absorb in the form of soup the products of their victims' decay. **❞**

—*Neltje Blanchan,* Wild Flowers Worth Knowing

blateration (noun | /blatəˈreɪʃən/): Incessant, foolish chatter. The start of this word, "blat," sounds too similar to other ugly words like splat, blot, and fart to ever be redeemed.

Origin: Sorry, blabber. You are *not* the father. Which is to say, *blateration* is not some blend of *blabber* and *conversation*, or anything else for that matter. It actually from the Latin *blaterare*, meaning "to blab."

❝ Blah, blah, blateration. I get it. ❞

—*Mean girl who has* really *been paying attention in her SAT vocabulary class lately*

blattnerphone (noun | /ˈblatnəfəʊn/):

Is there any word out there that actually looks good with "phone" tacked onto the end of it? Or was *blattnerphone* doomed from the very start? One of the first known recording devices in history, blattnerphones used steel tapes to record audio signals. The machines that would edit these recordings were so heavy and unrefined that they were known to shoot out razor-sharp metal if the spool fell off the track, giving blattnerphone operators one of the most dangerous jobs of the early 1920s and '30s. Next to, you know, mafiosos.

Origin: *Blattnerphone* actually hails from the name of its creator, Louis Blattner, a filmmaker who took his friend Kurt Stille's office-dictating machine and updated it for the mainstream market. So we can all blame Louis for this linguistic dumpster fire.

❝ I could not find my tape recorder so I decided to use my blattnerphone instead. **❞**

—*Emergency room patient explaining how they got a metal shard lodged in their belly*

blergh (exclamation | /blərg/): A nonsense expression used to articulate PG-13 frustration, popularized by Liz Lemon in NBC's *30 Rock*.

blister (noun | /ˈblɪstər/): Not to be confused with "B-lister," the term for the one-hit-wonder celebrity that you saw on *Dancing with the Stars* last week, *blister* refers to the fluid-filled sac that forms on your skin from intense friction or burning. The description alone, particularly "fluid-filled sac," is enough to ruin an appetite, but if you are still not convinced of this word's supreme ugliness, consider the "blist" at the front end. Doesn't saying it create the sensation that you are shooting little daggers out of your mouth? If you are into that sort of thing, cool, but maybe avoid parties or crowded spaces, okay?

Origin: Likely from the Old French word *blestre* meaning "lump" or from the Middle Dutch word *blyster* meaning "swelling." Could also have roots in the Old Norse word *blæstri* meaning "a blast."

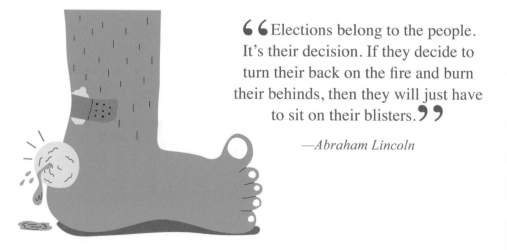

❝ Elections belong to the people. It's their decision. If they decide to turn their back on the fire and burn their behinds, then they will just have to sit on their blisters. ❞

—*Abraham Lincoln*

bodacious

bodacious (adjective | /ˌboʊˈdeɪʃəs/): Excellent, impressive, thorough, or (the definition you are probably thinking of) voluptuous. Aside from being an uncomfortable yet eloquent catcall you might hear on the streets of New York City or from the mouth of a creepy dinner date, bodacious is also the kind of word that would send a spittle flying out onto your friend's face mid-conversation thanks to the strong *b* and *d* at the beginning, making it gross on multiple levels.

Origin: Unknown, but probably a variant of the British word *boldacious* meaning "brazen" or a mix of the words *bold* and *audacious* with a dash of inspiration from the word *body* or *bootylicious* (which, outside of the Destiny Child's song, is simply unacceptable).

❝Sometimes when we label something dystopian fiction, I feel like we're trying very hard not to use the words 'science fiction,' because science fiction has those horrible connotations of rocket ships and bodacious babes.**❞**

—*Paolo Bacigalupi*

boil (verb / noun | /bɔɪl/): As a verb: the act of pushing a liquid to
its temperature limit, causing it to sizzle and turn into vapor. As a noun: a hard, swollen, pus-filled lump on the skin. The latter is the more problematic definition, as it usually brings to mind visions of ogres and trolls covered in chunky, cottage cheese boils caused by Lord-only-knows-what.

Origin: Taken from the old French *bolir,* meaning "to boil," and the Latin *bullire,* meaning "to bubble."

❝Hypocrisy is a boil. Lancing a boil is never pleasant.❞

—High Sparrow, Game of Thrones

bologna (noun | /bəˈloʊnjə/): Smoked, seasoned, sometimes sliced sausage that is easily the worst of the cold cuts.

Origin: Taken directly from Bologna, the city in northern Italy where this dish originates, this ugly word now belongs wholesale to the American Midwest.

> 66 Have you seen the bologna that has the olives in it? Who's that for? 'I like my bologna like a martini. With an olive.' 'I'll have the bologna sandwich—dirty.' 99
>
> —*Jim Gaffigan*

booger (noun | /ˈbʊgər/): The gooey mucus that comes out of your nose or the gooey creature that forms in your mom's uterus, slips out after nine months, quadruples in height, and eventually torments you on long family road trips.

Origin: A variant of *bugger* ("a contemptible person").

> 66 It's not how you pick your nose, it's where you put that booger that counts. 99
>
> —*Tre Cool*

boomie (noun | /bum-mi/): For those of you reading this and wondering "Oh, so like another word for a Baby Boomer?": you wish. The actual definition was invented by a less adored generation, the millennials, and it is just as bad as you might expect. Instagram has a spinoff app called Boomerang that allows users to take short, animated snapshots of an event. It is a hybrid of sorts, like the love child of a picture and a video, and it has become all the rage among young people, so much so that it has even gained the grossly preppy nickname, *boomie*. As if *Insta* wasn't bad enough on its own.

Origin: Instagram gave birth to Boomerang which gave birth to boomie who was definitely not born in the 1950s.

Hey_Bae_Bae

" Take a lit boomie of me hugging this tiger so I can totes post it on my Finsta. Don't worry, I'll give you photo cred. **"**

—*The worst humans*

bosom (noun | /ˈbʊzəm/):

To be clear, this word is not ugly because it has to do with the female body. This word is ugly because it looks like it is going to be pronounced like "baw-zum" or "bow-sahm," but then you see the pronunciation guide and realize it is actually "boo-zum" like the cry of a broken ghost.

Origin: Bosom has a history longer than your poetry professor's Gandalf beard. Though primarily from the Old English *bósm*, it also stems from Old Frisian (*bósm*), Old Saxon (*bósom*), Middle Dutch (*boesem*), Dutch (*boezem*), Old High German (*buosam*), Middle High German (*buosem*), and modern German (*busen*). Apparently, people loved bosoms so much, they wanted to make sure they were able to discuss them in pretty much every language.

❝ The best remedy for a bruised heart is not, as so many people seem to think, repose upon a manly bosom. Much more efficacious are honest work, physical activity, and sudden acquisition of wealth. ❞

—Dorothy Sayers,
Have His Carcase

bougie (adjective | /ˈbu(d)ʒi/): A wax candle; a thin surgical instrument used for probing passages of the human body; what your mom calls your neighbor Cynthia who only shops at Michael Kors and has three maids for her seven-bedroom mansion.

brexit (noun | /ˈbrɛgzət/): The withdrawal of the United Kingdom from the European Union, a decision that most of Britain regretted almost immediately. This departure was the result of the shocking vote taken on March 29, 2017, that granted the country the right to leave the EU, the metaphorical equivalent of a parent granting a child the right to run away from home with no food or water or feasible long-term financial stability plan. The term was so buzzy in 2017 that it secured the top spot on that year's list of "most obnoxious words." Considering the fact that brexit sounds like a five-tequilas-in frat boy's slurred attempt to correct you on politics, it is hard to disagree.

Origin: A smashing combination of the words *British* and *exit*.

> 66 Brexit was like the UK got drunk and accidentally unfriended Europe on Facebook. 99
>
> —*Leo Kearse*

bric-à-brac (noun | /ˈbrɪkəˌbrak/): Small decorative

items that one might see on the "miscellaneous" table at neighborhood yard sales. Author Edith Wharton once said that there were three "tiers" of household ornaments: *bric-à-brac* (knick-knacks), *bibelots* (trinkets), and *objets d'art* (art objects). Of course, those tiers have since changed to "things that spark joy" and "things that don't spark joy," per Marie Kondo.

Origin: First identified by lexicographer Émile Littré, who claimed the word was inspired by the French phrase *de bric et de broc* meaning "by hook or by crook." Others suggest that it was taken from the (similar) obsolete sixteenth century phrase *à bric et à brac* meaning "any old way."

❝ The thoroughly well-informed man—that is the modern ideal. And the mind of the thoroughly well-informed man is a dreadful thing. It is like a bric-a-brac shop, all monsters and dust, with everything priced above its proper value. **❞**

—*Oscar Wilde*

brine (noun | /braɪn/): Salty water. Like, *really* salty water. Seriously, imagine a cup of hot human tears. Now plop a large dill pickle in that cup, swirl some ocean water in there, and let it soak for a few hours. The result is probably pretty briny.

brobdingnagian (adjective | /ˈbrɒbdɪŋˌnag/):

Huge. Giant. Tremendously large. When someone told this word to go big or go home, it took it seriously in almost every way. And while the creative effort is appreciated, the excessive "dings" and "brobs" this word contains bring to mind teenage hooligans banging pots and pans on a crowded train. And for that, it gains a spot on the ugly list.

Origin: From Brobdingnag, the name Jonathan Swift gives to an island in *Gulliver's Travels* where everything exists on a gigantic scale. Members of this island are also known as Brobdingnagians.

> 66 Do you think this dress makes my butt look brobdingnagian? 99

buccula (noun | /ˈbəkyələ/):

As if the term *double chin* was not bad enough, doctors decided to invent an additional label for the lump of neck lard that consistently results in self-esteem-shattering Jabba the Hutt selfies. What's worse? It is pronounced "buh-cue-luh" which sounds like Dracula's voluptuous brother.

Origin: A play on the New Latin word *bucca*, meaning "small cheek." That's right. Buccula basically means "a rogue cheek that got lost on the way to your face and settled under your chin."

> 66 Fun fact about me? I have five cheeks. Two on my face, two on my butt, and one baby buccula. 99
>
> —*A winning Tinder profile*

bucolic

(adjective | /bjuˈkɑlɪk/): Pastoral; pertaining to country life; relating to shepherds. Not Jack Shephard from the hit TV series *Lost* or the German Shepherd from the puppy live stream playing on the local adoption center's Facebook page, but old-fashioned shepherds that round up sheep in the countryside.

Origin: From the Latin *būcolicus* ("relating to shepherds,") which was inspired by the Greek *boukolos* ("cowherd").

> **❝I can't come out, I'm, um, sick...
> with the...Bucolic Plague.❞**
>
> —*Your Definitely-Not-Sick Friend*

bulbous (adjective | /ˈbəlbəs/): Having or resembling a

bulb; bloated. Some bulbous items: dirt-caked vegetable roots, your old Uncle Stan's nose, the bulging eyes of your slightly sketchy next-door neighbor, and everyone's favorite "bulbous" Pokémon Bulbasaur—the only redeeming item on this grossly bulbous list.

Origin: Hails from the Latin *bulbus*, "pertaining to a bulb." Not much has changed since its first recorded use in 1578, it seems.

> **❝** I'm so sorry that I didn't want your rather bulbous head struggling to find its way through the normal size neckhole of my finely knit sweater. **❞**
>
> —*Jason Hanky,* Seinfeld

bulge

(verb / noun | /bəldʒ/): As a noun: a protuberance. As a verb: to swell. As a word: terrible in every context. Need proof? Fine. Scenario one: you are petting your neighbor's kitten Felix when you feel a small, hard bulge under your fingers, forcing you into a moral predicament: Do you peel apart the fur and risk finding a tick that you will inevitably have to remove for the safety of the cat? Or do you ignore the bump and pretend like it never happened, making you the person who potentially let a kitten get Lyme Disease? Scenario two: you are at a pet store and the owner hands you a baby pug with eyes so big, they look like they could burst at any moment. Would be cute, but the possibility of an eyeball explosion is just too strong. Scenario three: you are at the doctor, listening to him describe the pus-filled bulge on your tailbone to a group of medical students, when it suddenly bursts open, filling the room with a rank odor. Everyone suffers. Summary: *bulge* is the worst.

Origin: This word has been around for centuries, so its origin story runs deep. The noun version stems from the Old French *bouge* ("wallet") and the Latin *bulga* ("leather sack"). Some believe the word is a variant of *bulch,* meaning "a hump," or *bilge* meaning "bulging part of a military front." Others think it was influenced by *botch,* meaning "a swelling."

> ❝ His eyes are bulging like the belly of a hungry chaffinch. ❞
>
> —*Sid Waddell*

bunion (noun | /ˈbənjən/): An inflamed bony bump located on the inside of the foot at the big toe joint, causing mild discomfort and transforming you into the person who is always asking, "Have you seen my shoe inserts?"

burp (verb / noun | /bərp/): The release of gas from the digestive tract through the mouth. This loud, smelly gust of air is often used as a tool by television writers to quickly let the audience know that the character they're about to meet is rude, grimy, and probably hasn't bathed in a few weeks. (Case in point: Homer Simpson.)

Origin: It's hard to focus on the sound of a burp when the smell of a burp is so painfully stinky, but someone must've, because sources claim this word's origin is imitative.

" When birds burp, it must taste like bugs. "

—*Bill Watterson*

cack (verb / noun | /kak/): One of many (*many*) British slang words for "poop."

cacophony (noun | /kəˈkafəni/): If you ever find yourself standing before a towering shelf of bone China in a crowded dishware shop with an overwhelming need to create chaos, try something. Tip it over. The cacophony that ensues (aka, the discordant combination of sounds) should be enough to cure your morbid curiosity.

calculator (noun | /ˈkalkjʊˌleɪtə/): A device used to perform complex calculations or really any computation that involves using more than two percent of one's brainpower.

cankle (noun | /kæŋk(ə)l/): Ankles so thick that they appear to merge with the calf, making the two body parts indistinguishable.

cataract **(noun | /ˈkædəˌræk(t)/):** A clouding of the lens of the eye that obscures the vision; a waterfall that rushes over a precipice; a portcullis. The word has also been used to describe the "floodgates" of heaven, the ones that opened up a deluge and forced Noah to sit on a boat with a bunch of bickering animal couples for a few weeks.

catawampus **(adjective | /katəˈwɒmpəs/):** Destructive or askew. Has no relation to the shape-shifting Wampus Cat from American folklore or the magical group from the Ilvermorny School of Witchcraft and Wizardry that your Harry Potter–obsessed friend keeps badgering you about. "Have you taken the test on Pottermore yet??"

catheter **(noun | /ˈkæθədər/):** What's long and hard and hurts to stick up your urethra? A catheter, which is essentially a twisty straw that is jammed into the bladder of patients who cannot relieve themselves on their own.

caucus (noun |/ˈkɔkəs/): A closed meeting involving members

of the same political party during which they debate policy matters, select future candidates, and compare their favorite election memes. A mix between a cackle and a cough, this term needs to be abolished, along with male ponytails and ketchup-flavored foods.

Origin: A complete mystery. Some sources claim that this word was first used in Boston around 1724, but the term does not appear in any texts until 1763. There is a theory that *caucus* is a bastardization of the word *caulkers* meaning "meeting," but this idea has been repeatedly dismissed by many experts. Another theory points to the Caucus Club of Boston, a social club active during the 1760s whose name possibly stems from the Greek word *kaukos* meaning "drinking cup." Yet another theory says it comes from the Algonquian word *caucauasu* meaning "counselor." The one thing everyone can agree on? The fact that every other derivation of caucus is more pleasing than the word *caucus* itself.

❝I have learned the difference between a cactus and a caucus. On a cactus, the pricks are on the outside.❞

—*Mo Udall*

chafe

chafe (verb / noun | /tʃeɪf/): Friction caused by two objects rubbing against each other; a state of vexation or passion; what happens when you wear short shorts in the summer and the slim layer of sweat between your thighs irritates your skin, forcing you to spread your legs and hobble like a penguin for the remainder of the day to avoid a pain that is both uncomfortable and wildly inconvenient.

Origin: From the Middle English *chaufe-n* and the Old French *chaufer* meaning "to warm." Does this mean, then, that next time your crush says "my hands are cold," you can offer to "vigorously chafe" them to heat them up? No. That's weird. Don't do it.

> ❝ It's hard to find peace with your thighs, but when they chafe, try to be grateful for them. Your thighs let you run and get you where you want to go. I have not just thigh peace but thigh happiness, and it begins with thigh gratitude. ❞
>
> —*Margaret Cho*

chide

chide (verb / noun | /tʃaɪd/): To scold by way of criticism, as in "Mom chided Dad for his loyalty to a spineless political party built on fear-mongering and the perpetuation of racist ideologies, and for leaving the toilet seat up *for the third time*."

chork

(verb / noun | /ˈtʃɔrk/): *Chork* earns the distinction of having two very different yet equally terrible meanings. On one hand, it can refer to the combination of a chopstick and a fork, an invention made for the 96 percent of Americans who do not know how to use chopsticks. On the other hand, it can also refer to the squishing sound that your socks make when you walk around in waterlogged shoes. (See: *moist*.)

Origin: A distortion of the word *chark* which means "to grate one's teeth," likely because the sound of the term *chork* makes you want to do just that.

"The chork is the fork-chopstick love child that America deserves."

—*Real* Washington Post *headline written by one of the aforementioned 96 percent of chopstick-impaired Americans*

chortle

(verb / noun | /ˈtʃɔːt(ə)l/): The snort-chuckle that erupts from someone's mouth when they are laughing so hard, they are no longer able to control what they sound like and start hiccup-laughing like some Porky Pig–hyena hybrid. The only thing more disturbing than a chortle is chortle's pronunciation, which sounds like the name of a rejected Pokémon.

Origin: Coined by author Lewis Carroll in the 1871 *Alice in Wonderland* sequel, *Through the Looking Glass*. On page 24 of the original book, Carroll writes: "'O frabjous day! Callooh! Callay!' He chortled in his joy."

> **❝** The funniest line in English is 'Get it?'
> When you say that, everyone chortles. **❞**

—*Garrison Keillor,* We Are Still Married: Stories and Letters

chump (noun | /tʃəmp/): A lump of timber; the blunt end of an object; someone (usually a man) with an IQ lower than a piece of wood's.

chunky (noun | /ˈtʃəŋki/): *Chunky* (meaning "lumpy") is a word so vile, it can make even the most pleasant image sound disgusting. Let's try. Chunky flower. Chunky chocolate milk. Chunky Jonathan Van Ness. See? The *unk* in the middle, which you have to pull from deep in your throat, ruins everything, just like your uncle at every Christmas family gathering.

Origin: A variation of *chuck*, meaning a "block of meat" or "a large piece of wood used for burning."

" I travel the world, and I'm happy to say that America is still the great melting pot— maybe a chunky stew rather than a melting pot at this point, but you know what I mean. **"**

—*Philip Glass*

clammy (noun | /ˈklæmi/): Uncomfortable dampness. Can also be used to construct the unfortunate nickname Clamler, which you can use on any Tyler or Skyler you know who suffers from excessively clammy palms.

Origin: *Clammy* first appeared in the fourteenth century in the form of *claymy*, which is around the same time that the Middle English word *clam* popped up, suggesting an association between the two.

❝ Her skin is cold, and clammy; her eyes are the color of sky, on the grey, wet days that leach the world of color and meaning; her voice is little more than a whisper; and while she has no odor, her shadow smells mucky, and pungent, like the skin of a snake. ❞

—*Neil Gaiman,* The Absolute Sandman: Volume 1

clavicle

clavicle (noun | /ˈklavɪk(ə)l/): While clavicle *sounds* like one of Inspector Gadget's new claw-based gizmos, in reality, it just means "collarbone."

clog (verb / noun | /klɑɡ/): As a noun, a heavy piece of wood attached to a person or animal in order to impede motion. As a verb, to stuff something (like a bathtub drain, an artery, a dangerously small toilet) to the point of impeding motion.

clot (noun | /klɑt/): A small mass formed by the coagulation of a substance. Its consistent use in the medical field to refer to "blood clots" has ruined the term for life, a fact that the world seems to agree on considering there is not a single instance where clot has a positive connotation.

Origin: From the Old English *clott* ("a lump"). Also has roots in the Middle High German word *klotz* meaning "wedge or lump."

> ❝ A sentence that clots in your mouth is unlikely to flow in your mind. ❞
>
> —*Mal Peet*

clump

(verb / noun | /kləmp/): A thick, compact mass of things; to form a clump; to tread heavily in an attempt to bother the downstairs neighbors who like to file noise complaints every time you vacuum or breathe. *Clump* is the bigger, uglier version of *lump*, like the older brother that went off to college and gained the freshman fifteen.

Origin: From the Low German word *klump* or Middle Low German *klumpe* meaning "mass." No relation to the critically underrated *Nutty Professor* sequel, *Nutty Professor II: The Klumps.*

> **❝** You devious clump of overpriced fabric and hair product! **❞**
>
> —*Annie Edison,* Community

coagulate (verb / adjective | /kəʊˈagjʊlət/): To thicken
and congeal into a larger mass. As an adjective: being clotted. *Coagulate* mimics the sound of spit gathering in your throat, conspiring against you. If phlegm could talk, *coagulate* would be its favorite word.

Origin: Taken from the Latin *coagulare* meaning "to curdle," adding a gross etymology to this already gross word.

> **❝**If, for some reason your life functions ceased, my most precious one, I would collapse, I would draw the shades and I would live in the dark. I would never get out of my slar pad or clean myself. My fluids would coagulate, my cone would shrivel, and I would die, miserable and lonely. The stench would be great.**❞**

—*Beldar Conehead,* Coneheads

UDDERLY EXPIRED

coelom (noun | /ˈsiːlɒm/): The body cavity of metazoan

creatures that acts as a cushion, protecting the internal organs. However, is it clear that no one thought to protect the ears when they invented the word, considering how odd *coelom* looks and sounds.

coitus (noun | /ˈkəʊɪtʌs/): Have you ever read a book or a

TV script that says something along the lines of "Aimee and Roger cuddled postcoital" and wondered what it meant and why hearing it made you regurgitate part of your Cobb salad from lunch? Well, get ready. It means...wait, are your parents around? Can you double check? No? How about your younger siblings? Are you sure they're not eavesdropping? Can you go somewhere private just to be safe? Are you there? Here, come closer. Ready? This word means...stop giggling, this is important. This word means "intercourse." Yes, the thing humans have been doing for hundreds of years that no one seems able to talk about, forcing us to come up with gross euphemisms like *making love*, *shaboinking*, and *slaying the vadragon*.

Origin: Taken directly from the Latin *coitus* meaning "to go together," which is probably how your health education teacher described it on the first day of class.

> **"Coitus is random, children are definite."**
>
> —*Thomas Keneally*

congeal (verb | /kənˈdʒil/): To solidify; to change something from a fluid to a solid state. Basically, the opposite of what happens to every forty-two-year-old woman's legs whenever George Clooney walks by. The letters at the end of the word almost sound like they're coagulating together when you say them. Con-*geeeaaaal*.

Origin: Spanning back to the fourteenth century, *congeal* first found its roots in Middle English (*congele*) and Latin (*congelāre*, which is a mix of *con* meaning "together" and *gelare* meaning "to freeze"). Its association with dried blood and old crusty phlegm, though, is as old as time.

> 66 Blame, certainly, is a dish only edible when served fresh and warm. Old blames, grudges and scores congeal and curdle and cause the most terrible indigestion. 99
>
> —*Stephen Fry,* Moab Is My Washpot

corroded (adjective | /kəˈrəʊdɪd/): Eaten or worn away.

Runner-up for the "worst adjective to pair with *artery*" award, losing out to *clogged*.

---

cranny (adjective | /ˈkræni/): A small crack or crevice. One of

the many words your grandmother loves to use whenever you lose something.

Origin: Related to the French word *cran* meaning "a hole" or "a notch." At least, that's everyone's best guess. Some sources claim that errors made in transcribing this word back in the day make its true etymology hard to track, but those people sound just a little uptight, don't they?

> **❝ Have you checked all the nooks and crannies, my dear Pumpkin Face? ❞**
>
> —*my Nana*

crepuscular

(adjective | /krɪˈpʌskjuːlə/): Of or pertaining to twilight (not the teen romance book where twinkling vampires fall in love and a werewolf claims a literal baby as his soulmate but the other twilight: the hazy pre-evening period when the sky looks like cotton candy and bloodthirsty mosquitoes rise from their slumber to snack on you). Gross not only because the word "pus" is nestled in the middle but because it sounds like the love child of *crap* and *spectacular*.

Origin: Hails from the Latin *crepusculum*, "dusk." Its older form, *crepusculine*, is cuter and probably dated the hot quarterback in high school.

> 66 There's a country spread out in the sky, a credulous carpet of rainbows and crepuscular plants: I move toward it just a bit haggardly, trampling a gravedigger's rubble still moist from the spade to dream in a bedlam of vegetables. 99
>
> —*Pablo Neruda,* Pablo Neruda: Five Decades

crock (noun | /krɑk/): A earthenware pot; dirt; a debilitated person, animal, or object; a pet name a crocodile gives its lover.

croissant (noun | /ˈkwasñ/): These flaky French pastries aren't gross on their own. They only become gross when your aspiring cosmopolitan friend, who just returned from studying abroad in Europe, loudly announces their distaste for "American croissaints" in your local coffee shop, rolling their tongue as they say it like they are now the expert on all foreign baked goods.

cronk (noun | /krɑŋk/): The croak of a raven or wild goose. Not to be confused with Kronk, the loveable airhead from *The Emperor's New Groove*.

crotch (noun | /krɑtʃ/): In the agricultural sense, *crotch* refers to a fork used for handling weeds. In every other sense, it is a grating, vulgar slang word for one's genitals.

crusty (adjective | /ˈkrəsti/): Flaky or, more literally, crust-like. While crusty should be used to describe food (see: ***croissant***), more often than not, it is used to describe objects that are much less appetizing, like the dry skin caused by athlete's foot or the eye-boogers that harden on your lashes overnight.

Origin: From the Old French *crouste* and the Latin *crusta*, both meaning "crust" or "rind." Then someone added a *-y* suffix and everything went downhill from there.

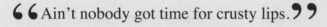

66 Ain't nobody got time for crusty lips. 99

—*Nina Agdal*

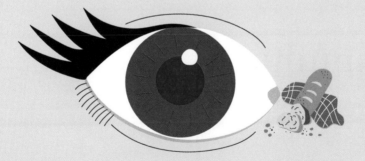

cummerbund (noun | /ˈkəmərˌbənd/): A

sash worn around the waist as a belt, sort of like that time in middle school when you tied the sleeves of your Scooby Doo sweatshirt around your hips really tight because your pants were too baggy and you were "too cool" to wear a real belt.

Origin: While this word looks like the name of a hummingbird's scandalous sister species, tragically, it's just a literal translation of the Persian word *kamar-band* meaning "loin-band."

> 66 A Dodger uniform just doesn't look
> good with a cummerbund. 99
>
> —*George Lopez*

cumulus (noun | /ˈkjuːmjʊləs/): Unfortunately pronounced

like "q-mew-luss," cumulus is a type of cloud that looks like snowballs piled onto other snowballs. Probably the kind of cloud your kid draws in pictures.

curd

curd (noun | /kərd/): When you leave milk out for more than a day, it goes sour. When you leave milk out for many days, the acids begin to force the milk into little lumps called curds. When you leave the milk out for many weeks, some turophile will take it, throw even more acid into it, and transform it into an obscure delicacy called "cheese." You have probably never heard of it.

Origin: What could possibly be worse than a word that sounds like another name for "lumpy turd"? A word that comes from the Middle English term *crud* meaning "any coagulated substance."

> **❝ Who spit in her bean curd? ❞**
>
> —*Grandmother Fa,* Mulan

custard (noun | /ˈkəstərd/): Sure, custard tastes delicious.

But don't you think it would taste slightly better if it were called something else? Something that didn't have "turd" in the name, perhaps?

Origin: A variant of *crustade*, a French, pie-like pastry made of eggs, herbs, and, according to the *Oxford English Dictionary*, flesh.

> 66 What sticks in my mind from seeing the *Teletubbies* is Tinky Winky's handbag and Tubby Custard. I always remember wanting to have a glass of Tubby Custard and some Tubby Toast in the morning. 99
>
> —*Daniel Rigby*

cwm (noun | /kʊm/): Meaning "a U-shaped gorge enclosed by

mountain walls," *cwm*'s bold choice to go vowel-free is infuriating to everyone who was raised on the singsong "A-E-I-O-U and sometimes Y" rule.

cyst (noun | /sɪst/): A thin-walled lump that develops abnormally on the human body and fills with semisolid liquid. As a prefix, *cyst-* refers to the bladder. *Cystectasy*? Dilation of the bladder. *Cystelminth*? A bladder worm. *CystGottaPee*? The sudden swelling of the bladder when the five jugs of water you drank at dinner hits you an hour and fifteen minutes into the movie you paid a month's worth of rent to see and you must bolt to the nearest bathroom.

Origin: Taken from the Modern Latin word *cystis*, "bladder-like bag," and the Greek *kystis*, "bladder or pouch."

> ❝ Just about everything in this world is easier said than done, with the exception of 'systematically assisting Sisyphus's stealthy, cyst-susceptible sister,' which is easier done than said. ❞
>
> —*Lemony Snicket,* The Hostile Hospital

debt
(noun | /dɛt/): What's easy to get, hard to lose, and can make a grown man cry? Answer: it's debt. Massive, debilitating debt.

dachshund
(noun | /ˈdakshʊnd/): A short-haired, long-bodied German dog breed. Also known as wiener dogs, dachshunds themselves are very cute. Their names, on the other hand, feel so deliberately convoluted as to inspire anger and disgust.

Origin: Taken from the German *dachs* ("badger") and hund ("dog"), the dachshund's name relates directly to their original purpose: to hunt badgers. Their long, thin bodies made it easy for them to burrow into the dirt and lie in wait for their prey.

> ❝ Dachshunds are ideal dogs for small children, as they are already stretched and pulled to such a length that the child cannot do much harm one way or the other. ❞
>
> —*Robert Benchley*

dank <small>(adjective | /dæŋk/):</small> Imagine something moist. Now imagine something cold, smelly, moldy, and unpleasantly moist. That, my friends, is dank. At least, that is the definition most adults use. If you are under the age of eighteen, dank can also refer to something cool or "lit." (Not sure what *lit* means? Wait a few pages, we will get to it.)

Origin: Uncertain, though we do know that the (now obsolete) verb form of this word ("to moisten") appeared almost a century earlier than the adjective and was probably borrowed from the Scandinavians or Germans.

> ❝They perfected a means of bringing to the surface all that was evil and negative within, erupting, spreading, connecting. In time, it formed a second skin, dank and vile!❞
>
> —*Voice of Armus,* Star Trek: The Next Generation

decay

(verb / noun | /dɪˈkeɪ/): To progressively decline; the result of a progressive decline. Things that decay? Neglected teeth. Rotting bodies. Overused sidewalks. Your sense of productivity the second someone says, "Hey, you want to watch that new Netflix thing?"

decrepit

(adjective / noun | /dɪˈkrɛpɪt/): As an adjective, worn out due to old age or overuse. As a noun, someone who is feeble, like your Great Aunt May who is on her third rewatch of *The Young and the Restless* and whose buttcheeks have left a permanent imprint on the couch.

Origin: From the French *décrépit* and the Latin *dēcrepitus*, which derives from the participle *crepāre* meaning "to creak." Considering how "creaky" our bodies get when we age, this origin checks out.

> ❝ The years between fifty and seventy are the hardest. You are always being asked to do things, and yet you are not decrepit enough to turn them down. ❞
>
> —*George Eliot*

defenestrate (verb | /diˈfɛnəˌstreɪt/): Made popular

by early Facebook users who used this "action" against their friends online before realizing it's not a dirty word and is actually just a bizarrely specific word for throwing someone out a window.

Origin: A sandwiching of the Latin word *fenestra* meaning "a small opening," the English prefix *de-*, and the English suffix *-ate*. It was born out of the 1618 incident where Protestants tossed two Catholic leaders out of a window in a heretical rage, kicking off the Thirty Years War and earning the fun historical name "The Second Defenestration of Prague."

❝ Expect defenestration, helicopter crashes, and exploding motorbikes. ❞

—*Vogue* editors describing what to look forward to in the next year's movie scene

diaper

(noun | /ˈdaɪ(ə)pər/): Disposable underwear worn by untrained babies. Boasting a feces-meets-industrial-plastic scent, diapers are both a blessing and a curse for their ability to catch poop and hold onto it until some poor soul catches a whiff of its contents and faints.

Origin: Taken from the Middle English *diapre* and the Old French *diaspre* meaning "patterned cloth." Likely also stems from the Medieval Latin *diasprum* meaning "white silken" and the Medieval Greek *diaspros* meaning "pure white."

> **❝** Roses are red. Violets are Blue.
> Will this diaper have pee or will it have poo? **❞**
>
> *—A joke you can write on a diaper*
> *to lessen the pain of changing it*

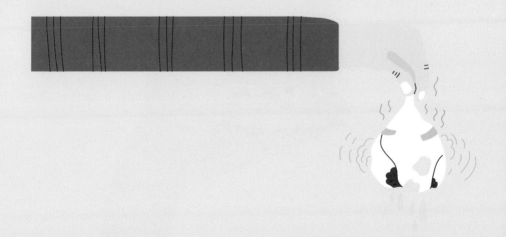

dinky (adjective | /ˈdɪŋki/): Embarrassingly small or dainty. Or, a rich professional couple with lots of money and no kids to spend it on. The latter would probably use the former to describe anyone who is not the latter, as in "Wait, *that's* your house? That dinky three-story mansion with *just* a drawbridge entrance? How sad."

Origin: From the Scottish slang word *dink* meaning "finely dressed."

> ❝I have this infantile fantasy that one day, I'll amount to something as an actress. A dinky little cottage in Cambridge? A playpen in the bedroom, diapers on the towel rack. How soon would it be before we started hating each other? How soon would it be before I started dashing out and disgracing myself at some nearest pub?❞

—*Sally Bowles,* Cabaret

diphthong

(noun | /ˈdɪpˌθɔŋ/): A monosyllabic sound where two side-by-side vowels are pronounced as one, like the "ea" in beard. To put it into context, this word is sort of like what happens in elementary school when you make your first friend and proceed to hang out with them so much that people start to refer to you both as a single entity. "Where is Drewcifer?" a teacher might ask. "Oh, they're playing tetherball, for the sixth straight hour," a concerned student might respond.

Origin: Predictably, this unusually spelled word is from the French, borrowed from the word *diphthongue*. It also hails from the Latin *diphthongus* and the Greek *diphthongos*. All of these involve combining *di-* (meaning "two") with *phthongos* (meaning "sound").

> 66 Round one of the spelling bee is on. Although if you're a big fan of Devon Zima, he just crapped out on a diphthong. 99

—*Frankie Bergstein,* Grace and Frankie

discharge (verb / noun | /ˈdɪsˌtʃɑrdʒ/): To release from a

particular state. Technically, this word has one more definition...but the details are sort of sticky, so we won't get into it. (If you really want to know, you may refer to the entries for **goop** and **panties**.).

Origin: Of multiple origins, including from the French *deschargier* ("to unload") and the Late Latin *discarricare* (*dis* meaning "to do the opposite of" plus *carricare* meaning "to load a wagon").

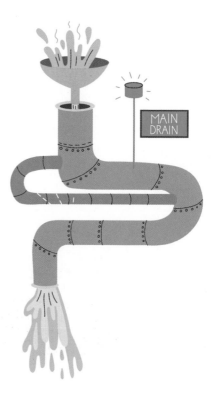

❝ In the discharge of the duties of this office, there is one rule of action more important than all others. It consists in never doing anything that someone else can do for you. ❞

—*Calvin Coolidge*, plainly admitting to a "Work Smart, Not Hard" philosophy

dollop (noun | /ˈdɑləp/): A blob of something, usually sour cream because Dollop of Daisy was a brilliant marketing scheme that seared the connection into everyone's brains and all those who worked on it should be proud.

dongle (noun | /ˈdɑŋɡəl/): Back in the 1980s, *dongle* meant "a software protection device which must be plugged in to be enabled." Today, dongle means "that little wire you plug into your iPhone one time and then immediately lose."

douche (noun | /duʃ/): A strong jet of water applied to certain body cavities as a means of cleansing, or a device used for this purpose. You probably saw it in a French Airbnb once.

drudgery (noun | /ˈdrʌdʒəri/): Work that is boring. Probably invented by someone who was tasked with creating a term for "impossibly dull and dreadful" because that's exactly how this word feels.

dumpster (noun | /ˈdʌmpstə/): A vessel that houses trash, grime, and those massive raccoons that like to sit outside your window at dinnertime and threateningly wring their hands, like villains in a cartoon.

encroach

(verb | /ɛnˈkroʊtʃ/): To gradually and sneakily advance. This word is ugly simply because it brings to mind approaching roaches. Literally, just an army of dirt-crusted creepy crawlies, headed right for you. Cue the bodily shivers.

Origin: From the Old French word *encrochier* ("to seize"), which makes sense, considering a cockroach's ability to seize the conversation whenever it slinks into a room.

66 Never give way to melancholy; resist it steadily, for the habit will encroach. 99

—*Sydney Smith,* A Memoir of the Reverend Sydney Smith: Volume 1

epidermis (noun | /ɛpɪˈdəːmɪs/): Skin. Pure,

unadulterated, peppered-with-so-many-pores-it-looks-like-TV-static skin.

epiglottis (noun | /ɛpɪˈglɒtɪs/): The flap at the root

of the tongue that automatically blocks the windpipe whenever food or drink is
ingested. Basically, a little skin door that stops you from choking.

eschew (verb | /əˈʃuː/): Bless you. What? Didn't you just

sneeze? Oh, wait, *eschew*. Got it. *Eschew* means "to avoid" or "to shun."

exoskeleton (noun | /ˈɛksoʊskɛlɪtən/): The hard

outer shell of invertebrate animals. Sort of like a human skeleton, except it's not
cushioned by blood or filled with gooey marrow.

eyeball

(noun | /ˈaɪˌbɔl/): The part of the body that allows humans to see; the round capsule containing the pupil and the iris. Eyeballs are not inherently gross if they are left inside the head. It is when you start imagining them on their own—round, wet, and full of liquid just waiting to pop open like an overfilled balloon—that eyeballs induce the heebie-jeebies. Just imagine a paddleboard, its ball dangling from a thin white strand. Now, replace the ball with an eyeball and the string with a set of slimy veins. Convinced yet?

Origin: *Eye + ball.* Easy eyeball peasy.

> ❝ That's what the internet is: it's like bombarding your eyeballs with these myriad blinking colour lights. It's like trying to watch a movie on your phone in the middle of Times Square. ❞
>
> —*Michel Gondry*

fart

(verb / noun | /fɑrt/): To blow intestinal gas out of the anus; the expulsion of said gas from the anus; a boring friend who insists on going home at 10:30 p.m. on a Friday night because they're "tired" and they "don't want to do eleven tequila shots on an empty stomach and vomit all over the dance floor." The last definition is usually paired with the word "old" (e.g., "old fart") because the only thing worse than a fresh fart is an old one that has been festering inside your body for a few hours.

Origin: Though originally from the Old High German *ferzan* ("to break wind"), fart has popped up in mythological stories all over the world, albeit in a different form: *fist*. One tale tells the story of Thor and the night he and his companions accidentally slept in the mitten of a giant. Afraid of the booming snores from the nearby sleeping monster, Thor was hesitant to even "fist" (aka, "fart") in the night. The vulgarity of this word made it popular across class and party lines, which explains its wide range of forms.

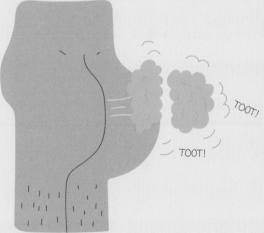

66 Can you think of a single situation, no matter how grave, where the atmosphere would not be instantly shattered with a loud fart or a drawing of a butt? There is no faster way to create universal common ground. 99

—*Euny Hong*

fecal (adjective | /ˈfiːkəl/): Poopy. A fancy word for poopy.

fecund (adjective | /ˈfɛkənd/): A regular adjective that means "fertile" and, surprisingly, isn't a curse word.

Origin: The French originally fashioned this word as *fecond* meaning "fruitful." Later, they realized that the Latin spelling, *fēcundus*, was much less appealing and decided to go with that instead.

> 66 *Fecundity* is an ugly word for an ugly subject. It is ugly, at least, in the eggy animal world. I don't think it is for plants. 99
>
> —*Annie Dillard*

fester (verb | /ˈfɛstər/): To build up over time. Often used in reference to a bulging, infected wound or a rapidly intensifying argument. There are only two ways that festering can end: in the formation of pus or in an explosive disagreement over work schedules that results in a resentful breakup or a trip to a marriage counselor. One is gross, one is ugly, both are uncomfortable.

Origin: From the Old French *festrir* ("to ulcerate") and *festre* ("a fistula"). Both terms stem from the Latin word *fistula* meaning "pipe" or "ulcer."

❝ Lilies that fester smell far worse than weeds. ❞

—William Shakespeare

fetid (adjective | /ˈfɛdɪd/): Foul-smelling.

Definitely not the kind of word that you would use to describe a rose garden or a fresh laundry pile or a newly bathed kitten. Think about it. If you saw a sign at the local adoption shelter that read "fetid cat," your mother would probably turn to you and say, "Why would they sell wild animals? That's not safe. I'm going to report them." And you would say, "No mom, you're thinking of *feral*. The poster said *fetid*." And she'd go "Really? Huh. Well it still sounds just terrible." And you would both walk away feline-free, before you even had the opportunity to give the Smelly Cat a chance.

Origin: From the Latin *fētidus*, meaning "stinking." And not in the "you're so stinking cute" sort of way.

> **❝** You can cut me off from the civilized world. You can incarcerate me with two moronic cellmates. You can torture me with your thrice daily swill, but you cannot break the spirit of a Winchester. My voice shall be heard from this wilderness and I shall be delivered from this fetid and festering sewer. **❞**
>
> —*Charles Winchester,* M*A*S*H

filth (noun | /fɪlθ/): Unclean matter; moral corruption; an insult that an angry female character hurls at her cheating husband as she shoves him out the door a few scenes before she embarks on her *Eat Pray Love* journey.

Origin: From the Old Saxon word *fūlitha* ("decay") and the Old High German word *fūlida* ("stench"), with influences from the Old Dutch word *fūlitha* ("moral corruption"). Originally, filth referred to decayed tissue within the body but when people started using it to describe human excrement, the term became fair game as a descriptor for anything considered "dirty."

> ❝ When the soul, through its own fault...becomes rooted in a pool of pitch-black, evil-smelling water, it produces nothing but misery and filth. ❞
>
> —*Saint Teresa of Avila,* Interior Castle

finstagram (noun | /ˈɪnˌstagræm/): Fake, meet

Instagram. Instagram, meet Fake. What a cute couple. Let's call you Finstagram. This, most likely, was the thought process behind this abominable moniker for someone's "Fake Instagram," aka, a second, private Instagram account reserved for a person's closest friends where they can post embarrassing or vulgar content that they might not want to upload to their public page. What's gross about Finstagrams are not the accounts themselves but the idea behind them. Teenagers should not feel pressured to create multiple social media pages catered to different friend subgroups. They have enough to deal with, like puberty and prom and choosing which expensive university they want to be eternally indebted to. They shouldn't have to add this to their already stressful balancing act.

Origin: The Finstagram seed was planted in our psyche long ago by that one friend who got a camera for Christmas, used it to take unflattering photos of just about everyone, and uploaded those photos to the internet without considering how the array of blackheads and visible chin hairs in said photos might affect the emotional stability of their owners.

❝❝I know you're like, mid-vom, but could you tilt your head towards the camera for one second? I'm curating posts for your Finstagram and this one will work perfectly.**❞❞**

—Your worst friend

flaccid

(adjective | /ˈflaksɪd/): Drooping or hanging loosely; limp; bending without elasticity; weak. The sound of a deflating eggplant emoji balloon or a sassy, disrespectful snake: "You are so flaccccccccccid."

Origin: Pulled directly from the Latin term *flaccidus*, meaning "flabby," and the French *flaccide*.

> **"**Oh, we are but soft and squishy bags of mortality rolling in a bin of sharp circumstance, leaking life until we collapse, flaccid, into our own despair.**"**
>
> —*Christopher Moore*

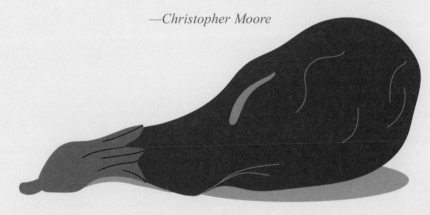

flatulence

(noun | /ˈflatjʊləns/): Flatulence was one linguist's attempt to beautify farts. Sort of like when you stuff fabric softener into your buttcrack so your gas comes out smelling more like a field of lavender and less like a poop-scented burp.

flesh

flesh (verb / noun | /flɛʃ/): As a noun: the soft, squishy part of the body enclosed by skin. As a verb: to provide more details about a subject, as if you were "fattening" the argument. The word *flesh* is acceptable only in the context of medicine. If a nonphysician uses this word outside the walls of an emergency room, it is because they are secretly a vampire picturing the feeling of your flesh between their teeth. There is no other explanation.

Origin: The history of this word is lengthy, but in essence, flesh comes from the Old English word *flæsc* meaning "meat," "living creature," or in rare cases "near kindred" (which explains the phrase "flesh and blood"). There are also connections to the Old Saxon *flêsk* ("flesh"), Old High German *fleisc* ("meat"), and the Old Norse *flesk* ("pork").

66 Your skin looks so flesh today. I mean fresh. 99

—*A vampire's Freudian slip*

fungus

fungus (noun | /ˈfəŋɡəs/): Defined as any type of spore-producing organism feeding on organic matter, a fungus is anything but fun. Part of the Fungi plant kingdom, fungus is often the cause of infections and invasive vegetation. It is frequently used in reference to foot fungus (an infection that thrives in the warm, sweaty space between your toes) and occasionally used in reference to mushrooms, but not the tasty kind that you sauté for dinner, the creepy grey kind that you find blooming in your garden despite your best efforts to prevent them. Fungus flanks the unpleasant *ungu* sound with *f* and *s*, thus slamming the reader with an unappetizing and rank word sandwich.

Origin: Fungus has been around since the 1520s and comes from the Latin word *fungus* meaning "mushroom," which is believed to be derived from the Greek *sphongos* for "sponge."

❝ Why did the mushroom go to a party? Because he's a Fungi! **❞**

—*A joke to tell at parties*

gash

(noun | /gæʃ/): A deep wound, the kind you would get after doing that one thing your mom expressly told you not to do. Usually accompanied by buckets of blood, a gash is painful to pretty much everyone, including the victim who receives it and the friends of the victim who are forced to look at it in the ambulance on the way to the hospital.

Origin: The love child of the Old French word *garse* ("an incision") and the word *slash*, according to most dictionaries and nine out of ten dentists.

" Tig's got a gash the size of your attitude on his leg. Got enough Advil for that? **"**

—*Bobby Munson,*
Sons of Anarchy

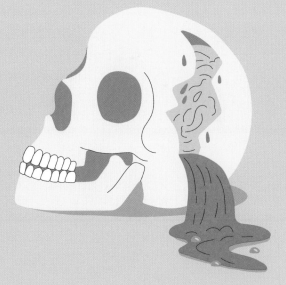

gassy (adjective | /ˈɡæsi/): Full of gas—not in an automobile sort of way, but in a my-boyfriend-ate-Mexican-food-and-has-been-farting-in-bed-all-night sort of way. Some sources theorize that wars could be fought more effectively through the use of butt gas over tear gas, though this has not been tested.

Origin: Many moons ago, alchemist and physician Paracelsus used the Greek word *khaos* to describe "the elements of the ancients." Later, in a book on medicine, Flemish chemist J. B. van Helmont used the term to describe a new vapor he found, swapping the Greek *kh* sound for the Dutch *g* sound, creating the word *gas*. Is this why spaces packed with fart gas are nicknamed Dutch ovens? Because the original wordsmith was Dutch? No, but wouldn't that have been fun?

❝Don't know if I'm elated or I'm gassy. But, I'm somewhere in that zone.❞

—*Princess Anna,* Frozen

gauze (noun | /gɔz/): A thin piece of fabric used to wrap wounds, meaning it's rarely ever *not* covered in blood, pus, or some other bodily fluid. Gross or gross?

Origin: Likely from the French word *gaze* meaning "regard." Like, "you're bleeding profusely from every orifice, you should probably pay some regard to that."

❝ They used to photograph Shirley Temple through gauze. They should photograph me through linoleum. ❞

—*Tallulah Bankhead*

geriatric (adjective | /dʒɛrɪˈatrɪk/): Relating to old people, especially ones named Gerry who play a lot of golf and won't stop leaving their dentures on the living room table.

Origin: *Geriatric* (the adjective) is borrowed from *geriatrics* (the noun), which is a branch of medicine dedicated to studying the health of old people and why, exactly, they continue to buy you products from infomercials for Christmas no matter how many times you tell them to stop.

❝ I refuse to spend my life worrying about what I eat. There is no pleasure worth forgoing just for an extra three years in the geriatric ward. ❞

—*John Mortimer*

gerrymander (verb | /ˈdʒɛrɪmandə/): To

manipulate the boundaries of a district in hopes of influencing political elections for a particular party. Not a fan of politics? Try this: Picture an elementary school classroom. Xander, a precocious ten-year-old, has been tasked with finding out what snack his classmates want for lunch. Xander wants pizza. However, only six of his classmates want pizza. The remaining nine want cake. Rather than report that nine is the majority, Xander breaks the class into three groups: Group A has five cake lovers. Group B has two cake lovers and three pizza lovers. Group C also has two cake lovers and three pizza lovers. Xander then polls the three groups. Group A votes for cake. Group B and C, though, have more pizza lovers than cake lovers because of how they were divided, so they vote for pizza, putting the final vote at one group for cake and two groups for pizza. Xander gets his pizza because Xander is a twerp and only cares about what Xander wants. And that's gerrymandering.

Origin: Back in the 1800s, a politician named Elbridge Gerry, fearing the rise of Federalism, signed a one-of-a-kind redistricting bill that ordered new state Senate district lines. These new borders favored the Democratic-Republican party over the Federalists. At a Federalist dinner party a few months later, someone began joking about the new districts, pointing out that one of them was so wildly misdrawn, it looked a little bit like a winged salamander. "No, a *Gerry-mander,*" another said. And the rest was history.

❝ No one likes the Electoral College, expect perhaps those who were elected because of it. No one likes gerrymandering, except those doing the gerrymandering. No one likes the filibuster, except those doing the filibustering. ❞

—Kevin Bleyer

gesticulate (verb | /dʒɛˈstɪkjʊleɪt/): Another word that

seems dirty but isn't (see: *masticate*), gesticulate simply means "to flail one's limbs dramatically while speaking."

gingivitis (noun | /ˌdʒɪndʒəˈvaɪdɪs/): The only thing

dentists love more than forcing you to talk about your flossing habits with their knuckles halfway down your throat is highlighting the many ways that your teeth can decay if you neglect to take care of them, usually through graphic brochures that you purposefully avoided looking at in the lobby. One of those brochures probably had a picture of gingivitis on it, which is an infection of the gums that causes them to inflame.

Origin: Classical Latin *gingīva* ("gums") plus the suffix *-itis*.

> ❝ Half of Americans suffer from gum diseases like gingivitis. Are you one of them? Schedule your next dental appointment to find out! ❞
>
> *—An intentionally anxiety-inducing ad*

gland (noun | /glænd/): An organ that secretes and discharges
chemicals or fluids from the body. The mere mention of this word brings to mind
images of sweat seeping out of the glands covering the skin and the rank body
odor that comes with that process.

Origin: From the French *glande* meaning "tumor." Which means you have full
permission to imagine the glands on your face as a minefield of microscopic
black tumors, waiting to ruin your day.

> ❝If you were to open up a baby's head—and I am not for a
> moment suggesting that you should—you would find nothing
> but an enormous drool gland.❞
>
> —*Dave Barry*

gleek (noun | /gliːk/): A card game where the goal is to collect three
of the same cards; a form of spitting that occurs while yawning; a trio; a joke or
trick; a nickname for any and all fans of the beloved Fox musical dramedy *Glee*.

glisten (verb | /ˈglɪs(ə)n/): To shine, but barely, like someone
took a damp rag and dragged it across your face, leaving a thin layer of moisture
that sparkles when the sun hits it just right.

globular (adjective | /ˈglɑbjələr/): Having a spherical
shape like a globe. Globular items include but are not limited to: a bald man's head, mouse droppings, an eye dangling from its socket, plastic balls from the McDonald's PlayPlace ball pit, the chunk of mucus that you coughed up three days into having the flu, and peas, aka, everything that makes you go "Ew."

Origin: From the Latin *globularis* ("spherical") and *globulus* ("globule"). Though *globule* and *globular* share the same Latin etymology, *globular* is used more often in association with *globe* than it is with *globule* which means "a small, round particle of substance."

66 This is Orson Welles, ladies and gentlemen, out of character, to assure you that *The War of the Worlds* has no further significance than as the holiday offering it was intended to be: The Mercury Theatre's own radio version of dressing up in a sheet and jumping out of a bush and saying 'Boo!' [...] Remember please for the next day or so the terrible lesson you learned tonight. That grinning, glowing, globular invader of your living room is an inhabitant of the pumpkin patch, and if your doorbell rings and nobody's there, that was no Martian, it's Halloween. 99

—*Next-level troll Orson Welles following the final*
War of the Worlds *broadcast*

gluten (noun | /ˈgl(j)uːtɛn/): A protein present in most wheat

products that helps foods maintain their shape, acting, if you will, like glue. If the thought of glue-soaked food or the guttural *glu* sound this word imposes does not gross you out, think about a graphic designer from San Francisco, probably named Chester or Maximillian, picking apart a restaurant menu for any trace of gluten—not for any medical reason, but because he wants to make condescending comments to the waiter about how food establishments refuse to accommodate healthier lifestyles. Repulsed yet?

Origin: We will make this one easy: it is from the Latin word *glūten*, meaning "glue."

> **"** Guys, there's only one thing I hate more than bloggers who start sentences with 'guys'—and it's those mealy-mouth hipsters who crochet codpieces and their ye-olde-sideburned friends who pickle stuff and slaughter their own gluten-free goats. **"**
>
> —*Jill Soloway*

GLUTEN-FREE

glutton (noun | /ˈɡlʌt(ə)n/): You know that feeling when
you've eaten so much food that your stomach, groaning in pain, feels like it's ripping at the seams? That's what gluttons feel like *all the time*. This select group of people enjoy eating to excess, a practice so unnatural, it was named one of the OG sins.

goop (noun | /ɡup/): Goop can mean one of three things: a sticky
semifluid gunk of any kind, a stupid person, or a "modern lifestyle" website that sells $15,000 sex toys and vampire repellent. (You know the one.)

Origin: Unclear, but it would not be unreasonable to think that some parent came up with it after realizing the word "goop" made their kid laugh.

"Poop goop!"

—*Babies*

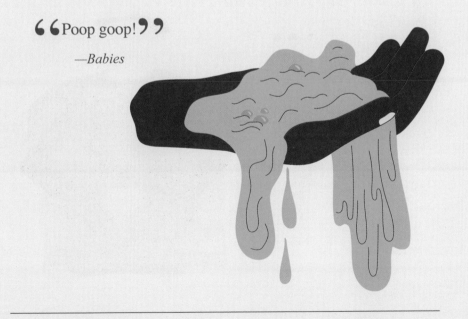

groin (noun | /grɔɪn/):

In the olden days, *groin* meant a number of things including "a snout," "a grumble," and "a seat of lust." These days, it is more commonly known as "the area between the lower abdomen and the upper thigh," aka, "the place where the family jewels live." The word *groin* sounds like the noise someone would make when they are in excruciating physical pain. Like Shaggy's "yoinks" but for real, 3-D people.

Origin: There is an Old English word *grynde* meaning "depression in the ground" that many link to this word, though it is unconfirmed. Most likely, it came from the Middle English term of the same spelling, *grynde*, meaning "groin."

> 66 Never raise your hand to your kids. It leaves your groin unprotected. 99
>
> —*Red Buttons*

grope (verb | /groʊp/): To search uncertainly with one's hands. Or, to search very certainly with one's hands in places where they most certainly should not be.

grub (noun | /grəb/): Both a nickname for insect larvae and a slang term for appetizing food that someone with no concept of what appetizing means likely created.

gubernatorial (adjective | /ˌgubərnəˈtɔriəl/): Relating to a governor or governorship in the United States. Not a suggestion that a "goober" is holding "national" office, or anything of the like.

gunk (noun | /gəŋk/): Any type of unpleasantly sticky substance. So, for reference, anything that feels like it was doused in Dr. Pepper the day before and left to dry, giving it a tacky texture.

gurgle

(verb / noun | /ˈgə:g(ə)l/): To make an airy, bubbling sound; the act of gurgling or the noise made by the act of gurgling. Whether it is a gurgling sink, a gurgling stomach, or a gurgling gargoyle hiding under a bridge readying for attack, nothing associated with this gassy burble suggests that you're about to have a good time.

Origin: Possibly from the German *gurgeln* ("to gargle"), the Italian *gorgogliare* ("to bubble up"), the Portuguese *gurgulhar* ("to gush out"), or the Latin *gurguliāre* ("gullet") but no one really knows for sure if it was directly inspired by one of these terms or if someone just heard their brother gargling soda at the dinner table and thought "That kind of sounds like 'gargle,' doesn't it?"

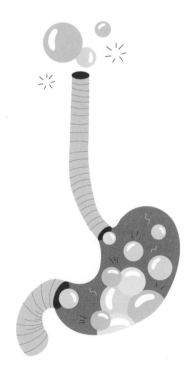

❝ Almost nobody believes anymore that infants are insensate blobs. It seems both mad and evil to deny experience and feeling to a laughing, gurgling creature. **❞**

—Paul Bloom

gusset (noun | /ˈgəsət/): An elastic addition to the side of a
boot; a triangular insert sewn into a piece of clothing to provide increased support or reinforcement, usually in the crotch area of jeans so we do not all have to waddle around in public like constipated penguins. Often used to refer to the little patch at the bottom of a woman's underwear, the part the family dog chews on to everyone's dismay.

Origin: From the Old French word *gousset*, meaning "armhole." Some sources trace the word back to *gousse*, a word of unidentified origin meaning "shell of a nut." How does this relate to the current definition? Unclear.

> **❝**I have always bought my socks and pants at Marks & Sparks. I've noticed something very troubling has happened. There's no other way to put this: their pants no longer provide adequate support. When I've discussed this with friends and acquaintances, it has revealed widespread gusset anxiety.**❞**
>
> —*Jeremy Paxman*

guttle (verb | /ˈgʌt(ə)l/): To greedily devour. It is what most people
do with their extra-large popcorn as they enter the dark, judgment-free movie theater.

hairball (noun | /hɛ(ə)rbal/): A disgorged ball of hair known to clog shower drains, sinks, and cat throats everywhere. Nothing gets under the skin more than the thought of lifting a moist clump of black follicles from the hole in the bathtub, not knowing how long it has been there or if it has formed a heartbeat already.

Origin: Take a guess.

> **"** I'm afraid I have to expel a rather ferocious hairball. You're on your own, girl. **"**
>
> — *Cheshire Cat*

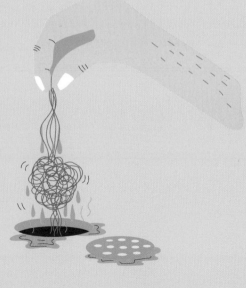

harangue

(verb / noun | /həˈræŋ/): A long, pompous, sometimes aggressive speech, or the act of giving such a speech. What a baby thinks an orangutan is called.

hogwash

(noun | /ˈhɑɡˌwɑʃ/): Nonsense of any kind; cheap liquor; kitchen scraps used to feed pigs. Legend has it that the sound of hogwash sloshing into a bucket has been used as a torture mechanism in the American Midwest for years.

hollow

(adjective | /ˈhɑloʊ/): Having an empty space; lacking in significance. Even the word hollow feels hollow, like you're speaking into a cave and hearing the echo of your own voice.

hornswoggle

(verb | /ˈhɔːnswɒɡ(ə)l/): To bamboozle. Most likely invented by a swashbuckling pirate who slurred this word whilst drunk and thought it sounded cool.

hubby

(noun | /ˈhəbi/): At some point in time, there was a woman who hated her husband's guts but didn't want the rest of the world to know. So, she went out with him, probably to some gala or company potluck, and described, through clenched teeth, how much she loves her "wubby dubby hubby" to anyone who would listen. And all the housewives nearby nodded as they took in this story, all while internally flinching at the sickeningly sweet moniker this woman had used to refer to her husband. And they have not stopped flinching since.

Origin: Apparently, that point in time was the 1680s, when this word first entered the universe as a common colloquialism and nickname for husband.

> ❝ My hubby is such a sneaker king...and I am a stiletto queen! He always wants to see me in sneakers, but I believe I can do anything in heels. ❞
>
> — *Khloé Kardashian*

icicle (noun | /ˈaɪˌsɪk(ə)l/): A dangling rod of ice formed from frozen trickling droplets. It's cold, it's sharp, and it will probably kill you if you stand too close to it. What's not to love?

ictic (adjective | /ˈɪktɪk/): Meaning "abrupt," *ictic* produces a sensation similar to that of a fly trying to run a marathon on a blob of sap. Which is to say, it's unpleasant.

idiot (noun | /ˈɪdiət/): A simple or uneducated person. Ugly because, well...it's just plain mean.

impale (verb | /ɪmˈpeɪl/): To stab with a sharp object like a stake or a dagger. For more information, see *Buffy the Vampire Slayer*.

impugn (verb | /ɪmˈpjun/): To dispute or oppose an argument that
one finds invalid or incorrect. For example, someone might impugn the spelling of *impugn*. Like, why is there a silent *g*? Who voted for that?

inbred (adjective | /ˈɪnˌbrɛd/): This word means "produced by
inbreeding" and is commonly used as a you-married-your-cousin brand of insult.

infection (noun | /ɪnˈfɛkʃən/): The corruption of the blood or
body, which often leads to illness and long weekends in bed surrounded by used tissues and Emergen-C packets.

Origin: Mostly from the Middle French *infeccion,* meaning "a putrid change of various substances due to a number of causes" including lack of hygiene or the disequilibrium of humours (think the old-fashioned bodily humors, not the string of bad jokes you dished out at open mic night last week).

> **❝**I sing and play the guitar, and I'm a walking, talking bacterial infection.**❞**
>
> *—Kurt Cobain*

insatiable (adjective | /ɪnˈseɪʃɪəb(ə)l/): Nothing should

ever be described as insatiable. Not a woman. Not a vampire. Not a hunger for a chilled bowl of rocky road ice cream with pieces of toffee and melted fudge on top. Nothing. Why? Because it sounds like the word you would use to describe either a ravenous animal or a sex-crazed maniac, neither of which are pleasant.

Origin: From Old French word *insaciable* meaning "ravenous" and the Latin word *insatiabilis* meaning "unable to be satisfied."

" Just after I entered my teens I suddenly entertained an insatiable enthusiasm for the delightful habit of criticizing others. **"**

—*Loretta Young*

irregardless (adjective | /ˈɪrɪriˈgɑrdləs/): Synonym

for *regardless*. Like the Easter Bunny, America's dignity, and your love for your grandmother's prune juice recipe, it does not exist.

Origin: Who knows? Most likely, some prepubescent boy defiantly tweeted "irregardless of ur stance, i luv President Carter's new album #kanye #respect" one evening, mistaking "irregardless" for "regardless" and birthing this grammatically incorrect phrase into existence.

> 66 Irregardless, ex-boyfriends are just off limits to friends. I mean that's just like the rules of feminism. 99
>
> —*Gretchen Wieners,* Mean Girls

jaundice (noun | /ˈdʒɑndəs/): That thing that happens in
medical dramas where the patient looks in the mirror to find that their face has
turned a troubling shade of yellow overnight. It occurs when waste material builds
up in the body, and it is just as gross as it sounds.

jawn (noun | /dʒɑn/): An all-purpose nonsense word loved by
Philadelphians, loathed by everyone else.

Origin: In 1981, the Bronx hip-hop group Funky Four Plus One released their hit
single "That's the Joint," sparking a wave of *joint* slang across New York. Philly
residents, envious of their neighbor state's fun new word, invented their own:
jawn. What does it mean? Anything you want. Like, literally anything. Hungry?
Get a *jawn* at the Wawa. Where do you live? Oh, in a tiny little jawn. What's your
name? Jawn.

> **❝❝** Jawn is the jawn and will always be the jawn. **❞❞**
>
> —*Some Philly person*

juice (noun | /dʒus/): When used to describe liquid extracted from
fruits and vegetables, *juice* is a perfectly reasonable word. When used to describe
other watery substances, like *eye juice* for tears or *cow juice* for milk, *juice*
becomes an abomination that should be banned from every English-speaker's
vocabulary.

junk (noun | /dʒəŋk/): Junk has a wide range of meanings, including:

any type of discarded waste with little or no value; a rush (a waterside plant with thin leaves); an old cable used for making gaskets; a category of food that all parents hate; a botched baseball pitch; or everyone's favorite, male genitalia. Anyone whose mother has ever screeched "put away your junk or it is going in the trash where it belongs" can attest that this word is ugly.

Origin: The 1400s marks the first known report of this word, which hails from the Old French *jonc*, the Spanish *junco*, the Portuguese *junco*, the Italian *giunco*, and the Latin *juncus*, all meaning "rush."

> ❝ My favorite review described me
> as the cinematic equivalent of junk
> mail. I don't know what that means,
> but it sounds like a dig. ❞
>
> —*Steve Buscemi*

kitschy (adjective | /kɪtʃi/): In poor taste due to excessive
garishness or tackiness. What you might call the section of your grandmother's
living room that's blanketed in collectible windmill statues.

Origin: Kitsch is actually a straight-up German word meaning "trash," which
pretty much sums it up.

> 66 At its core, kitsch feels like something less than art;
> it panders to the middle and is flagrantly anti-art, though
> it often apes or references art. This referential, ersatz
> quality is why it's so fun to collect. 99
>
> —*Carrie Brownstein*

kludge (noun | /kluːdʒ/): In computing, a system that has been
hastily thrown together. Think of it like that moment when your dad bursts into
your bedroom and asks what you've been doing and you glance around frantically,
trying to piece together an explanation for the loud thumping he's been hearing for
hours because you don't want to tell him that you've been reenacting scenes from
Jurassic Park by yourself, so you end up lying and saying you were practicing
how to use a hammer, or something. That's a kludge.

kraken (noun | /ˈkreɪkən/): A mythical Scandanavian sea

monster that's tall, dark, and known for snacking on unassuming sailors. It's also the gagging sound that your cat makes when it starts choking on the live mouse it just swallowed.

Origin: Though stories about this monster date back to the twelfth century, the name for it didn't appear until the publication of Carolus "Carl" Linnaeus's *Systema Naturae* in 1735, where he pegged it as a member of the cephalopod mollusk group.

> ❝ The kraken stirs. And ten billion sushi dinners cry out for vengeance. ❞
>
> —*Terry Pratchett*

krug (noun | /krʊg/): It's no surprise that this word means "beer mug"

because it sounds like the kind of nickname a person seven krugs deep would invent before initiating a keg stand and blacking out in the bushes.

Origin: Hilariously, *krug* is the German word for "jar." Why is this funny? Because it means the Germans can look at any container, even a plain ol' jar, and view it as another receptacle for beer.

> ❝ Give...me...that kitschy...mug...krug...thingy. ❞
>
> —*Likely an Oktoberfest slur*

kumquat (noun | /ˈkəmˌkwɑt/): An olive-sized citrus fruit native to south Asia that boasts a spongy rind and plump acidic pulp. Surpassing its brother the mandarin orange in utility, the kumquat is one of the only citrus fruits that you can eat whole, skin and all. Would you *want* to gnaw on a sour peel and bite into the dripping, saccharine core of this thumb-sized fruit with a name that sounds like a painful yoga pose?

Origin: Taken directly from the Cantonese word *kin kü* meaning "gold orange."

> **❝❝** If you turned the runes on their heads they revealed a spell to make your enemy's ears into kumquats. **❞❞**
>
> —*J. K. Rowling,* Harry Potter and the Order of the Phoenix

larva

(noun | /ˈlɑrvə/): You know those translucent, creepy-crawlies that horror films like to splice in shots of to rattle all the bug-averse viewers? Those are larva. (Or rather, *larvae*, in its plural form.) They are wingless grubs that go through several molts before blossoming into full-grown insects destined to terrorize innocent civilians.

Origin: *Larva*, the Latin word for "ghost," first appeared in the 1650s in Roman stories about ghouls and goblins. In these stories, specters often wore disguises so that they could blend in with the living, inspiring a second definition of this word: mask. Later, in the eighteenth century, naturalist Carl Linnaeus ran with this new definition. He used it to describe the early stages of animals because of how different they looked from their adult counterparts, as if these immature creatures were "masking" their regular bodies with these younger-looking shells.

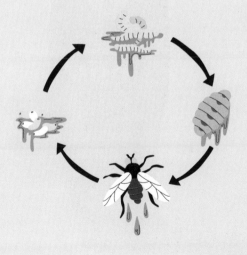

66 What's more gross than a fungus gnat larvae? Thousands of fungus gnat larvae swarming together to look like a giant blob snake. 99

— Gizmodo writer Casey Chan describing a human-sized pack of larvae on the sidewalk

leech (noun | /liːtʃ/): A carnivorous freshwater worm historically used by medical professionals who believed leeches could suck diseases out of a patient's body; someone who clings to another person for their resources or emotional support, sucking the victim, their bank account, and their sanity dry like their slimy animal counterpart.

Origin: Strangely enough, leech originally meant "a physician" or "a veterinary practitioner," drawing from the Old English root of the word *lǽc* meaning "strong." This likely contributed to the second definition, due to the believed healing properties of the bloodsucking water worms. However, the *Oxford English Dictionary* argues that the existence of another Old English form of the word (*lyce*) indicates that the worm version of leech may have been its own distinct term.

❝ No, Karen, you cannot have my Hulu password. I let you live at my house rent-free for four months, played Catan with your idiot friends in the kitchen every single night, and talked you down from the ledge after the landlord nixed your raised garden idea. Stop being a leech. ❞

—A frustrated friend/leech victim

latrine (noun | /lə'trin/): A low-grade, communal outhouse usually found in barracks. Also a deceivingly normal way to describe a big ol' hole filled with feces.

lice (noun | /laɪs/): Wingless, parasitic insects that feed on human blood. Not to be confused with your ex.

lickspittle (noun | /lɪkspɪd(ə)l/): A slimy subordinate who would do anything to impress the person in power, like murder a pesky coworker or lick their spittle off the cold hard ground.

lipid (noun | /'lɪpɪd/): An organic compound containing fatty acids that prevent it from dissolving in water. It's the reason why you can't wash the slick layer of olive oil off your hands, no matter how much water you splash on them.

lit **(noun | /lɪtʃ/):** The past tense of "to light"? Or a cringeworthy slang word concocted by seventeen-year-old boys who felt the word *cool* wasn't cool enough? Unfortunately, the answer is both. *Lit* in modern terms refers to a situation that is exciting and hip, like the high school cheerleader's mansion party or Donald Glover's latest music video or really anything that might contribute to someone's "wokeness."

Origin: *Lit* as a slang word has been around since the 1900s, though back then, it meant "intoxicated," as if alcohol and drugs had the ability to make people "light up with happiness." In recent years, the hip-hop scene has embraced this word, expanding its meaning from "a person who is lit" to "a place where lit people are." Travis Scott in particular has ushered in this new definition by dropping the line "it's lit" into so many of his songs that it is now considered one of his trademark phrases.

❝ This Christmas tree is lit, fam. No, for real. I plugged in the lights and everything. **❞**

—*A festive young adult*

literally

(adverb | /ˈlɪdərəli/): Ugly for its ability to induce frustration in any self-respecting English speaker, the word *literally* means both "in a literal manner" and "well, not *literally*." The word *literally* has been misused so often ("If I do not get a mocha frappuccino sprinkled with coconut strips in the next minute, I will *literally* murder the first barista I see!") that it has now adopted another definition: "virtually." In the second case, literally is used to provide emphasis, as in "I'm so hot I am literally melting." Are you, Vanessa? Are you melting?

Origin: A combination of *literal* (from the late Latin *literalis* meaning "belonging to letters or writing") and the suffix -*ly*.

> **❝** Screw them. Yeah. But not literally. I'm not advocating promiscuity. **❞**
>
> —*Mark Hoppus*

loogie (noun | /ˈlugi/): A lump of phlegm. Not the brother of video game star, Mario.

Origin: Appeared in the 1990s. Possibly borrowed from the word *lung*, as in, "What's that pink glob of spit in your hand? Did you just cough up a piece of your lung? An itty bitty lungie? A smooshy wooshy loogie?"

> 66 To truly hock a loogie, one must not retrieve the phlegm from the throat, but from the soul. 99

—*Snotty,* Revenge of the Nerds II: Nerds in Paradise

lozenge (noun | /ˈlɒzɪndʒ/): What you suck on when your throat hurts and you need a distraction from the snot slugs slinking out of each nostril.

lubber (noun | /ˈləbər/): A clumsy fellow. Frequently used by sailors as a nickname for bumbling seamen or landsmen.

Origin: Derived from the Old French word *lobeor* meaning "swindler." Long ago, *lobeor* developed an association with the slang term *lob* mean "bumpkin," which explains *lubber*'s negative connotation.

> 66 Nobody is so heartily despised as a pusillanimous, lazy, good-for-nothing, land-lubber; a sailor has no bowels of compassion for him. 99

—*Herman Melville,* Omoo: A Narrative of Adventures in the South Seas

lugubrious
(adjective | /l(j)uːˈgjuːbrɪəs/): *Lugubrious* sounds like the name of Eeyore's long-lost brother, like a glob of snot that grew legs and dragged its dribbling body into the One Hundred Acre Woods, leaving behind a trail of odorous sludge in search of his pouty donkey kin. Considering Eeyore's permanent gloom and lugubrious's true definition—mournful—it would check out.

Origin: *Lugubrious* hails from the word *lugubriosity* which comes from the Latin *lūgubris* ("of or pertaining to mourning").

66 The cello is not one of my favourite instruments. It has such a lugubrious sound, like someone reading a will. 99

—*Irene Thomas*

maggot (noun | /ˈmæɡət/): A type of insect larva found in

decaying organic matter. They feed on rotting food and, yes, dead flesh, but not as much as horror movies will have you believe. Also, an archaic name for a magpie or a whimsical or perverse notion (i.e., "That idea is so insane, there must be maggots in your brain!"). In sum, what sounds like a homophobic remark and evokes visions of bloodsucking bugs? This atrocity.

Origin: From Old English word *mathe*, which inexplicably evolved into the Middle English *maddock*. The term also stems from *Margot*, the (thankfully obsolete) pet name for Margery and Margaret back in the day.

❝If I hadn't just been sitting in it, I'd say you've lost your mind.❞
—*Maggot, Tim Burton's* Corpse Bride

malignant (adjective | /məˈlɪgnənt/): Petition to

rename every Disney villain "Malignant" (which means "malevolent") is a go.

marrow (noun | /ˈmɛroʊ/): A soft, fatty substance located at

the center of bones that produces blood and feeds the obscenely rich at five-star restaurants.

masticate (verb | /ˈmæstəˌkeɪt/): To chew food.

Masticate is inherently ugly for its similarity to a certain personal activity. For this reason, it (and anything that sounds like it) should be kept far, far away from any conversation involving food to avoid sending confusing images through the listener's brain. Like, if someone said, "Robert is violently masticating in the cafeteria," what would you picture? Survey says, it is probably not lunch-related.

Origin: Either a back-formation of *mastication* ("the act of masticating something") or from the Latin *masticare* ("to chew").

> **❝ Nature will castigate those who don't masticate. ❞**
>
> —*Horace Fletcher, solidifying* masticate's *unfortunate false connection with* masturbate

meal (noun | /mil/): The word for "a customary gathering involving food" that feels entirely unappetizing and sounds like an eel struggling to introduce itself. "Me, eel."

mealworm (noun | /ˈmilˌwərm/): The larvae of any
darkling beetle, particularly those of the Tenebrio genus. With small, rod-like bodies and khaki-colored skin, mealworms look like the most uninspired animated twigs that God could whip up. It almost makes you feel bad for fish, who are frequently lured to their deaths by fishermen using these buggers as bait. After all, when it comes to gravestone inscriptions, it does not get much worse than "death by worms."

Origin: Mealworms are used to feed everything, from fish to birds to adventurous foodies who are desperate to switch up their dinner routines. They are, you might say, a universal meal. But why are they called worms when they are actually beetle larvae? Simple. They look like worms.

> 66 [IKEA] has released five new dishes made from sustainable ingredients such as spirulina, beetroot, hydroponic sprouts—and mealworms. The insect items include 'Neatballs,' a re-imagining of the famous Swedish version, substituting mealworms for meat, and 'Bug Burgers.' 99
>
> —CNBC Reporter Ali Montag

meaty (adjective | /ˈmidi/): Everyone has a type. For some, it is
"tall, dark, and handsome"; for others, it is "cries at home renovation shows and
can only lift small dogs." For a select few, it is "meaty." What does that mean? In
dictionary terms: being full of substance. In layman's terms: any guy that looks
like he plays rugby and could be a Beater in a game of Quidditch. This preference
is perfectly acceptable; the nickname for it is not. Nothing, especially a body
type, should be described as "meaty" unless it is a literal, edible slab of meat.
Would you ever call someone's figure "granola-y"? Or "grape-y"? Or "key lime
pie-y"? No? Exactly. Because comparing human flesh to food raises cannibalism
concerns and it should be avoided at all costs.

Origin: Meat comes from the Old English word *mete* meaning "food item," and
-y is, well, a suffix. Put the two together, and you get an adjective. Welcome to
our weird language.

> **❝**Oh man, I can just taste
> those meaty leading man
> parts in my mouth.**❞**
>
> —*Tobias Funke,*
> Arrested Development

mildew (noun | /ˈmɪlˌd(j)u/): A white fungus that forms on
damp organic material like clothes or rugs. Commonly found in old apartment
complexes under that light fixture that always leaks when it rains.

milieu <small>(noun | /mɪlˈju/):</small> A word for "social environment" that seems impossible to say without sounding like a pretentious Frenchman.

milquetoast <small>(noun | /ˈmɪlkˌtoʊst/):</small> Picture a piece of bread. Now, dunk it in some milk. Now, leave it there. After a few days, the soggy bread will have dissolved into the sour milk, fusing with the curdled chunks to create a bitter, lumpy liquid that could take down even the strongest heroes. Fortunately, that is not what milquetoast is, but that gross image is certainly what comes to mind when you say it out loud. In reality, the word describes nothing more than a meek, submissive person.

Origin: *Milquetoast* does not actually describe milk toast, but it was inspired by it. In 1924, H. T. Webster, in his attempt to invent a character for his comic strip *The Timid Soul*, drew a picture of a man he called Caspar Milquetoast. This soft-spoken, afraid-to-offend figure was portrayed as plain and inoffensive, akin to "milk toast" itself, a meal which was often eaten by sensitive people with "weak" stomachs. People like Caspar Milquetoast.

❝ Quit pouting, girl. All a Milquetoast ever gets is wet. **❞**

—*Kristin Hannah,*
Home Again

moist (adjective | /mɔɪst/): Slightly or moderately wet; damp;

the linguistic equivalent of stepping in a lukewarm puddle in socks and feeling the water ooze between your toes with every step thereafter. Can also be used to describe particularly fresh baked goods, but only if you want to immediately ruin the appetite of anyone about to consume said baked goods.

Origin: From the Old French *moiste* and Latin *mucidus* meaning "moldy." Influenced by *musteus*, "fresh," from *mustum*.

> ❝ I'm gonna bake a cake so moist, girls are gonna be like, 'Ewww, why did you say moist? I hate that word!' and I'm gonna be like, 'Taste the cake!' And they're gonna be like, 'D—, it's moist! ❞

—*Coach,* New Girl

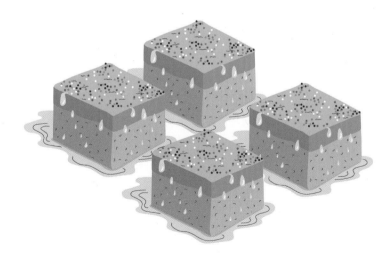

moisturizer (noun | /ˈmɔɪstʃəˌraɪzər/): A
cosmetic used for adding moisture to the skin? Or a weapon Dr. Who might use to drown his victims in lotion? You decide.

mollusk (noun | /ˈmɑləsk/): An invertebrate within the
Mollusca phylum. They have soft, shapeless bodies and thrive in cold, damp places like all of your greatest enemies.

molt (verb / noun | /moʊlt/): The act of shedding one's exterior; to
shed one's exterior, like a snake shedding its skin or a slimy politician shedding his lizard suit at the end of a long campaign.

mothball (noun | /ˈmɔθˌbɔl/): A clump of pungent
materials used to keep moths away from valuables and not (fortunately) a ball of dead moths as the name suggests.

muckraker (noun | /ˈmək͵reɪkər/): A person (or an institution) who investigates and publicizes evidence of corruption. Invented to describe the American journalists who attacked big businesses and scandal-ridden figures during the Progressive Era. It's a good thing we don't have to deal with anything like that in our current society.

mucus (noun | /ˈmjukəs/): Gooey substance secreting from mucous membranes, typically those found in the nasal passages. *Mucus* sounds like an ill person's attempt to say Marcus, but they cannot because their nose is plugged with mucus. Mucus looks like the slimy blob creature from *Ghostbusters* that, instead of terrorizing a library, terrorizes your nostrils. Mucus feels like you inhaled a pre-chewed piece of bubble gum and it got lodged so far up in your nose, it touched your brain. Mucus sucks.

Origin: Borrowed from the Latin word *mucus*, "slime."

❝ Oh Master, I love you, but I hate all that you stand for! But I think we should press our slimy, mucus-covered lips together in the cargo hold. ❞

—*HK-47,* Star Wars: Knights of the Old Republic

muktuk (noun | /ˈməkˌtək/): Whale blubber.

mulch (adjective / noun | /məlʃ/): Loose dirt-like material consisting of shredded wood and decaying leaves, used as insulation for plants and fake currency for children on every playground in America.

Origin: From German, somehow, likely from the modern German *mölsch* meaning "soft" or "rotten."

mullet (noun | /ˈmələt/): A type of edible fish; a star with five points; tweezers; an Atlantic puffin; a hairstyle commonly worn by men in the 1980s in which the hair is short on the sides, long in the back, and guaranteed to exude a serial killer vibe.

Origin: Yes, The Beastie Boys have brought a lot of great things into this world, but they also helped popularize this term, referencing a "mullet-head" in Volume 2 of their *Grand Royal* magazine back in 1995, and for that they can never be forgiven.

musk (noun | /məsk/): A type of aromatic substance used as a base in perfumery. Or, a reddish-brown odorous substance secreted by the glands of male deer. If only we could bottle up that scent....

nagware (noun | /ˈnægwɛ(ə)r/): A word almost as annoying as the definition itself, *nagware* refers to a computer software that is free for a trial period but hits you with constant reminders about the benefits of the paid version until you inevitably cave and buy it or until the trial period ends.

nashgab (noun | /ˈnæʃˌgæb/): A gossipy person.

nausea (noun | /ˈnɔziə/): Believe it or not, there's a word for that queasy rumbling you get in your stomach as you stare into the dizzying abyss of your toilet following a night of heavy partying or cheap Thai food: nausea. If you're feeling "nauseated" or "nauseous" and think that your situation can't possibly get any worse, just know that you can (see: *vomit*).

Origin: From the Latin word of the same name, meaning "seasickness."

❝ There is a very fine line between love and nausea. **❞**

—*James Earl Jones*

Nth (adjective / noun | /ɛnθ/):

In math, *nth* refers to an undefined variable in a series. In conversation, *nth* represents another way to say "extreme." In real life, *nth* is a pathetic excuse for a word. It is the door stopper of the English language, not long enough to feel satisfied that the word has escaped your mouth but not short enough to disqualify it as a dictionary entry. The good news? It counts in Scrabble.

Origin: In 201 AD, Greek mathematician Diophantus of Alexandria attempted to create a how-to guide to algebra by writing a thirteen-book series called *Arithmetica*. Though riddled with unusual mathematical approaches and few actual solutions, the collection went on to become one of the most important Greek texts at the time. Later, in 1575, professor William Xylander decided to translate the text into German. At one point, he encountered a portion of the text that required him to choose a new letter to represent an unknown value. He went with *n*. A few decades and a suffix later, *nth* was born.

❝ Have you seen the eight live reindeer standing on the Klaus's lawn? They celebrate Christmas to the nth degree. **❞**

—*A jealous neighbor*

nubbin (noun | /ˈnəb(ə)n/): A word to describe any not-fully-formed appendage or item, like Voldemort's nose or the little toe stub left behind when you accidentally sawed off half of it in your dad's woodworking shed on a hot summer afternoon.

nubile (adjective / noun | /ˈn(j)uˌbaɪl/): A strong, confident woman of marriageable age who apparently needs a man. Also, the creepiest synonym for "attractive."

nudnik (noun | /ˈnʊdnɪk/): An irritating or boring person. The title your coworker Nik gave to himself after spending three weeks "connecting with his body" at a nudist summer camp.

nuptial (adjective / noun | /ˈnəp(t)ʃ(ə)l/): Of or relating to marriage; a wedding; a potentially pleasant word ruined by its similarity to "nipple."

oaf (noun | /oʊf/): A large, bumbling man, and the only word in a seal's vocabulary.

ogre (noun | /ˈoʊɡər/): The green, man-eating monsters from folklore that have big heads and even bigger farts.

ointment (noun | /ˈɔɪn(t)m(ə)nt/): A paste or unguent used for cosmetic or medicinal purposes. Can also be used to puncture the eardrums of one's enemies (its harsh *t* sound, oinT-menT, can easily be weaponized) and to befriend the pig clique at parties by telling them bad jokes ("What does a pig use when it gets hurt? OINKMENT!").

Origin: From the Old French *oignement* ("salve"). The *t* came from the past participle of the French word *oindre* ("to anoint"). The pig joke above probably came from someone's **avuncular** relative.

SCAB-B-GONE

66 Ointment. That's what you need when your head's been cut off. That's what I gave your sister Mary when they done her. 'There, there,' I said. 'You'll soon grow a new one. 99

—*Nursie*, Blackadder

ooze (verb / noun | /uz/): To display some characteristic or quality.

To exude or pass through slowly, like tree sap dripping through the tiny holes in a strainer or lava creeping down the side of an active volcano or your confidence seeping out of every bodily orifice when a small glob of spit from your mouth lands on your crush's face mid-conversation. As a noun, any thick liquid with a sluggish flow. For those born in the 1990s/2000s, yes, the inside of a Gusher is the perfect example. What's more? *Ooze* may be the only word that feels like it is "oozing" from your mouth when you speak it aloud. Go ahead. Say it.

Origin: Derives from the Old English word *wase* meaning "soft mud" and the Middle English *wos/wosen* meaning "juice or sap." Cognate with the Middle Low German *wose*, "scum." No wonder this word feels so dirty.

66 You ever notice you can only ooze two things?
Sexuality and pus. Man, I tell ya. 99

—*Creed,* The Office

orifice (noun | /ˈɔrəfəs/): An opening, usually in the body, through which something may pass or, more commonly, through which something may attempt to pass and get stuck, resulting in a costly trip to the emergency room and an embarrassing lecture from the on-call nurse about what should and should not be shoved up each orifice. The word itself sounds like the next stage in the evolution of an ogre. Like, if Shrek could level up, he would morph into an Orifice. Cool for Shrek. Gross for everyone else.

Origin: Partly from the Middle French *orifice*, partly from the classical Latin word *ōrificium*, partly the reason you struggle to sleep at night.

❝ If I could smoke from more than one orifice, I most certainly would. ❞

—Graham Parker

ort (noun | /ɔ(ə)rt/): An uneaten scrap of food, and the sound of a wannabe hiccup.

palimpsest (noun | /ˈpæləm(p)ˌsɛst/): *Palimpsest*,

which refers to a material on which writing has been erased to make room for later writing, looks like the love child of *pimple* and *cyst* that was left in the back alley of a Chinese food restaurant and raised on the streets by a bunch of literal subway rats.

Origin: Thankfully, *palimpsest* actually has nothing to do with pimples or cysts: just paper. It was originally derived from the Latin *palimpsestus* ("paper which has been written on again") and the Greek *palimpsestos* ("scraped again").

> ❝Look at the blogosphere—the biggest lavatory wall in the universe, a palimpsest of graffiti and execration.❞
>
> —*A. C. Grayling*

pamper (verb | /ˈpæmpər/): To lavish with attention and food,

like what dads do to their babies or sugar daddies do to their sugar babies.

panties

panties (noun | /ˈpæn(t)iz/): A woman's undergarments and contender for worst word on this list next to ***moist*** purely for its consistent pairing with the word "used," as in "used panties" and as in "with no time to spare and no other option, I threw on a pair of used panties and charged out into the summer heat, fully aware of the stench that would rise from my crotch over the course of the day."

Origin: Interestingly enough, for all the flack women get for their "panties," this word was first attributed to men back in 1805. The derogatory term was transferred to women in 1908 with Mary Ella Morgan's publication of *How to Dress A Doll* and later in 1952 with the introduction of the phrase "panty raid."

❝❝ I'm secure enough in myself to wear panties with bows on them. ❞❞

—*Ilona Andrews*

paste (verb / noun | /peɪst/): A moist, semifluid, don't-get-any-on-your-hands-or-you'll-regret-it substance.

penetrate (verb | /ˈpɛnəˌtreɪt/): To enter or pass through something through force. Usually associated with one of two things: violence ("the knife penetrated the skin") or sex ("the eggplant emoji penetrates the peach emoji to make a baby emoji"). Used by immature punks, annoying younger brothers, and grandmothers who do not know any better.

Origin: From the Latin *penetrāre* ("to get into" or "to have insight into").

> **❝** You can't penetrate beyond society's sick, gray, fear of the flesh. **❞**
>
> —*Seth Brundle (aka Jeff Goldblum),* The Fly

phlegm

(noun | /flɛm/): Slimy mucus that coagulates in the throat. Phlegm is the source of the viscous frog in your windpipe that you tap into whenever you want to say the word *phlegm*, making this word a double whammy of disgusting.

Origin: A split etymology, from the Old French *fleume* and the Latin *phlegma*. Before phlegm became known for clogging the throats of kids and adults everywhere, it was widely recognized as one of Hippocrates's theorized four humors of the body along with blood, yellow bile, and black bile. Each "humor" informed a person's health—if one of the humors was imbalanced, it would be reflected in that person's behavior. According to the theory, an excess of phlegm (the cold and moist humor) resulted in an apathetic and sluggish person, a description that was upheld in the modern word *phlegmatic* meaning "of an emotionless disposition."

> 66 Escargot is French for 'fat crawling bag of phlegm.' 99

—*Dave Barry,* Dave Barry's Only Travel Guide You'll Ever Need

pierce (verb | /pɪ(ə)rs/): To penetrate the surface of something.

Things that pierce include hunting daggers, sharpened toothpicks, harpoons, and that cute barista's cerulean blue eyes.

plump (verb / adjective | /pləmp/): Sure, plump—which

means "having a round, filled-out shape"—can be used to refer to things like grapes. But we all know that is not why it is in this book. Plump is commonly used to describe female body parts like breasts or buttocks or bellies, usually by catcallers or inappropriate bosses. These predatory associations make the word feel ickier than it already was, and that says a lot about a term that looks like a pee-dump hybrid and sounds like that hybrid plopping into a toilet bowl.

Origin: "But plump can also be a verb for adjusting a pillow!" you say. "It was never intentionally negative." Get ready to stand corrected. The adjective comes from the Middle Dutch term *plomp* ("blunt, stupid") and the Middle Low German *plomp* ("clumsy"). The verb (which appeared even earlier, around 1400) means "to land heavily" (suggesting heft) and hails from the Dutch and German word *plumpen* (literally, "to fall with a plumping sound").

> **"I'm not fat, I'm festively plump."**
>
> —*Eric Cartman,* South Park

polyglot (noun | /ˈpäliˌglät/): A person who writes, speaks, or understands more than one language, and brings it up every couple of minutes with little or no prompting.

pore (verb / noun | /pɔ(ə)r/): To gaze intently; an opening in the surface of the skin; the bane of most acne-prone teenagers' existence. Blocked pores lead to blackheads which lead to whiteheads which lead to pulsing pimples and the swift termination of any romantic interaction you were hoping to have. The strong *p* in pore and the mouthful of air released when you say it mimics the sound of popping acne and pus oozing out, resulting in major nausea.

Origin: Directly from the Latin *porus* ("pore"), the Greek *poros* ("pore"), and the Old French *pore* (you guessed it, "pore").

> **❝** Good God, I can see every line and pore in your face. It looks like a YMCA climbing wall. **❞**
>
> —*Jack Donaghy,* 30 Rock

porpoise (noun | /ˈpɔrpəs/): A type of small whale

characterized by a small, round snout. This word might be nice if it didn't sound so much like some subpar actor's attempt to say "purpose" in an indiscernible accent.

Origin: Mostly from the twelfth century Old French word *porpais* meaning, and this is true, "pig fish." (That's right, Jessica Simpson. There isn't a chicken of the sea...but there is a pork of the sea.) This word has many other roots, including some from German, Latin, and Italian, but nothing beats the horrid image of a muddy pig slithering through the water.

> **❝** No good fish goes anywhere without a porpoise. **❞**
>
> —*Lewis Carroll*

porridge (noun | /ˈpɔrɪdʒ/): Boiled cereal or oatmeal. Boring

to the taste and even more boring to the ears.

Origin: Variant of *pottage*, meaning "a thick stew."

> **❝** This porridge is delicious! **❞**
>
> —*Goldilocks's last words before she was presumably devoured by the bear family whose home she had so casually broken into*

porta potty

(noun | /ˈpɔrdəˈpɑdi/): Porta potty. It is the to-go bathroom that sounds like it was named by an eighteen-month-old toddler, the waste hot box that mars the memory of every outdoor event you have ever attended, the poopy punchline of the low-budget comedy that your dad forced the family to watch on Thanksgiving, and the steamy plastic panic room always devoid of toilet paper and breathable air. The worst part? We need porta potties because without them, life would be infinitely crappier.

Origin: During the 1940s, thousands of men all over the country were prepping for the Second World War. Many had to spend long hours by the shore building boats. The problem? Most of these stations were ill-equipped in the bathroom department, forcing the workers to spend a significant amount of time walking back and forth from the docks to the nearest toilet. As a result, the crew members began to build "portable potties" to increase workflow efficiency. Two decades later, in the 1960s, a man named George Harding put a patent on these blue strong boxes, popularizing them by transforming them into the smelly receptacles we have today.

> ❝ Wow! That porta potty was roomy, well-lit, equipped with the right amount of hand soap, and did not smell like one thousand human derrieres. Would highly recommend! ❞
>
> —*A Yelp review you will never find*

potpourri (noun | /ˌpoʊpəˈri/): A collection of plants, herbs, and spices used to perfume a space. Might as well be called "poo-pretty" because we all know potpourri's true purpose is to eliminate the stench of feces in every hotel lobby bathroom.

Origin: From the French *pot pourri* meaning a dish of mixed meats. This idea of a "medley" was later applied to plants, leading to the potpourri's modern definition.

66 One man's toxic waste is another man's potpourri. 99

—*Jim Carrey*

protrude (verb | /prəˈtrud/): To stick out. Hated for all the times it has been used to describe noses.

pube (noun | /pjub/): What's small and dark and can destroy a restaurant's reputation with a single appearance? That's right! It's pubes! The thick, wiry hairs that live in your nether regions.

Origin: Taken from the Latin *pubes* meaning "grown up." Forget having an ID; the surest sign of adulthood is growing a couple of these puppies.

66 Dude, pube art is like back in a big way. 99

—*Adam DeMamp,* Workaholics

puce (adjective | /pjus/): A purplish, brownish, ugly-ish color.

pucker (verb | /ˈpəkər/): To tightly squeeze the edges of something together into an *O* shape. The sound you hear right before your great aunt Susan kisses you on the lips in front of everyone.

pulchritude (noun | /ˈpəlkrəˌt(j)ud/): Beauty, apparently.

Origin: Despite looking like a French insult for an ugly person, this term actually comes from the Middle French *pulcritude* and the classical Latin *pulchritūdō*, both meaning "attractive."

> **❝** Pulchritude—beauty where you would least suspect it, hidden in a word that looked like it should signify a belch or a skin infection. **❞**
>
> —*Zadie Smith, who gets it*

pulp

(noun | /pəlp/): The small, wet substance that forms the inside of most fruits. Or, a popular text or genre of text that is poorly written or "lowbrow." Both definitions are repulsive, but for different reasons. The former because there is nothing more nauseating than watching pulp flakes swirl around at the bottom of an unshaken orange juice carton, ready for you to guzzle and get lodged in your teeth. And the latter because it incorporates the works of New Pulp authors like E. L. James. This word is Fifty Shades of Get Out of My Vocabulary.

Origin: Pulp (the food) comes from the Latin *pulpa* ("animal or plant pulp"). Pulp (the genre) comes from the wood-based fibrous pulp paper that the original lowbrow stories of the 1920s were published on. *Pulp Fiction* (the movie) comes from Quentin Tarantino. All pulped out yet?

❝❝I like my music with all the rinds and seeds and pulp left in.❞❞

—Tom Waits

puncture

(verb / noun | /ˈpəŋ(k)(t)ʃər/): To pierce with a sharp object; a perforation. The hard *c* sound bisecting *puncture* creates a jabbing sensation in your mouth, as if a doctor were guiding a needle into the flesh behind your uvula and giving it a light prick.

Origin: From the Latin *punctura,* meaning "penetration by a pointed object." The transitive verb form did not appear until 200 years later and was derived directly from the noun.

> **❝**I am a disaster magnet. I came home from our first anniversary vacation with jellyfish stings, a puncture wound from a wrought iron pineapple, and a cork-shaped bruise in my cleavage.**❞**
>
> —*Molly Harper*

pungent (adjective | /ˈpəndʒ(ə)nt/): Painful; piercing;

having a sharp taste or odor. You can find this word listed under "terms that should never be used to describe your significant other."

pupil (noun | /ˈpjup(ə)l/): The opening of the iris through which the

light passes. Or, a student. Or, what a toddler would hear and call a poop pill which, honestly, almost sounds more appealing.

Origin: The definition of *pupil* as "student" came from the Old French term *pupille* and from the Latin *pupillus,* both meaning "orphan." The definition of pupil as "iris hole" came from from the Latin *pupilla* ("girl-doll"), supposedly because of the little reflection one sees when they stare into another person's eyes.

66 Time is a great teacher, but unfortunately it kills all its pupils. 99

—*Hector Berlioz*

pus

pus (noun | /pəs/): A thick, greenish-yellow liquid that forms as a result of an infection and, according to the *Oxford English Dictionary*, consists of "dead and living phagocytes [...] and other cellular debris." In other words, it is the glob of dead matter that bubbles under the the skin and causes extreme pain until you suck it up and burst it open, releasing the creamy goop into the world. It is a notch better than feces, a tad worse than blood, but firmly in the realm of awful.

Origin: Here is an easy one: *pus* comes from the Latin *pūs* meaning "viscous matter from a sore." It is also distantly related to *puter* ("rotten") and *putere* ("to stink").

> **"**I cry a lot. My emotions are very close to my surface. I don't want to hold anything in so it festers and turns into pus—a pustule of emotion that explodes into a festering cesspool of depression.**"**
>
> —*Nicholas Cage*

putrid

putrid (adjective | /ˈpjutrɪd/): Decaying to the point of emitting a rotten smell, like the banana that you left in your backpack or the egg that you stole from the fridge and snuck into your bedroom in hopes of watching it hatch only to see it spoil and cause a stink (both literally, when it starts to smell, and metaphorically, when your mom finds out and bans you from the kitchen).

Origin: From the French *putride* meaning "(of a fever) caused by putrefaction" and the Latin *putridus* meaning "rotten." Also a direct result of someone sniffing expired milk and going "P-UUUUUUU."

> ❝ I do not think myself to be a worm, and a grub, grass of the field fit only to be burned, a clod, a morsel of putrid atoms that should be thrown to the dungheap, ready for the nethermost pit. ❞
>
> *—Anthony Trollope*

putz

putz (verb / noun | /pʊts/): To dillydally or someone who dillydallies. Looks like the inscription a sixth grader would scribble in marker on the outside of their binder in an attempt to be quirky and fun. As in, "I putz my goodz in this bin-dizzle."

quaff **(verb / noun | /kwɑf/):** To drink with enthusiasm (or the act of doing so). Often results in throbbing hangovers and a lot of missed calls from some guy named "Hot Anthony."

queasy **(adjective | /ˈkwizi/):** Nauseated. The "kweez" at the start of "queasy" is enough to make someone, well, queasy.

queef **(verb / noun | /kwif/):** A sound that erupts from a woman's nether regions that is so disturbing, it can temporarily destroy her confidence with a single toot. Pair that with its spelling, which looks like a botched form of *queen*, and you have a recipe for disaster.

Origin: Have you ever listened to a queef? It sounds like "queef." Fittingly, that is where the word came from. Onomatopoeia strikes again.

66 *Geernt.* Sounds like a queef on a yoga ball.**99**

—*Kate Ellis,* Sisters

rancid (adjective | /ˈrænsəd/): Having an unpleasant taste or smell as a result of being rotten or old. Just imagine being locked in a windowless room with a slab of raw fish for a few days, and you'll get the gist.

raw (adjective | /rɔ/): Uncooked. Used in association with bloodied meat found at the butcher shop or in a serial killer's basement.

reek (verb | /rik/): As a verb: to stink. As a noun: smoke, a disturbance, an unpleasant stench, a lingering association, a hint of something corrupt, or a particular person slash *Game of Thrones* character who encompasses all of these qualities.

Origin: Originally meaning "smoke" or "odor," this word has roots in just about every language under the sun, including Old Frisian, Old Dutch, Middle Dutch, Old Saxon, Middle Low German, Old High German, Old Icelandic, Old Swedish, and Old Danish. Considering these origins all appeared before the invention of the shower, is it really a surprise that the word *reek* was so common?

> ❝I had the lunchbox that cleared the cafeteria. I was very unpopular in the early grades. Because I hung out with my grandfather, I started to bring my lunchbox with sardine sandwiches and calamari that I would eat off my fingers like rings. I was also always reeking of garlic.❞
>
> —*Rachael Ray*

regurgitate (verb | /rəˈgərdʒəˌteɪt/): To eject
or expel, usually from the stomach or mouth. (Fact: the sound of the word
regurgitate has been known to cause regurgitation in some listeners.) Also, to
repeat thoughts or ideas without thinking, like most of the outspoken high school
classmates or old relatives that you have unfollowed on Facebook.

Origin: Earliest known meaning is "to overflow," formed from the classic prefix
re- ("back") mixed with the Late Latin *gurgitare* ("engulf"). It developed a
second meaning, "to surge," as the past participle of *regurgitare*.

66 People regurgitate the
same old cliches and it
becomes like a photocopy of a
photocopy of something that's
vaguely interesting. 99

—*Steve Coogan*

roach (noun | /roʊtʃ/): A wall-scaling, human-scaring insect uglier
than an animate turd and crunchier than your favorite breakfast cereal.

rural

(adjective | /ˈrʊr(ə)l/): Meaning "of the countryside," *rural*'s definition is not actually gross. Its foulness stems more from its pronunciation, which forces the speaker to make a noise akin to the grunt of a zombie. The deep *u* sandwiched between *r* and *r* force all of the sounds to blur together, creating this growl-like tongue-twister.

Origin: From the French *rural* meaning "of or belonging to the country as opposed to a town or city," rural was often used interchangeably with *rustic* in the early days of its existence, as both refer to elements of the country and share semantic similarities.

> **❝** Now 'The Rural Juror' is a true story of Roy Jurner, who's pure furor ensures a terrible murder. **❞**
>
> —*Barbara Walters,* 30 Rock

salami (noun | /səˈlɑmi/): What's red and white and dead all over? This type of sliced, Italian meat.

salivate (verb | /ˈsalıveɪt/): To secrete saliva in response to something pleasurable, like food or a photo of a powerful woman in a pantsuit.

salubrious (adjective | /səˈlubriəs/): Conducive to one's health like, for example, anything other than the sound of the word *salubrious*.

Origin: In an insalubrious turn of events, get ready to take a year off your life for how boring the salubrious etymology is. The word comes from the Latin *salūbris*, meaning "health."

> 66 My health and spirits had long been restored, and they gained additional strength from the salubrious air I breathed, the natural incidents of our progress, and the conversation of my friend. 99
>
> —*Victor Frankenstein,* Frankenstein

sauerkraut (noun | /ˈsaʊəˌkraʊt/): Fermented cabbage

that is an unfortunate staple of the German diet. No offense to the Germans—your reputation for perfection is well-regarded—but you may have gotten this one wrong. Not (solely) because of its acrid taste but because of your trademark complicated vowel combination that creates the impression the speaker is reeling in pain: "S-OW-er-kr-OW-t."

Origin: A blend of the German words *sauer* ("sour") and *kraut* ("vegetable").

> **❝** Three wars back we called sauerkraut 'liberty cabbage' and we called liberty cabbage 'super slaw' and back then a suitcase was known as a 'Swedish lunchbox.' Of course, nobody knew that but me. **❞**
>
> —*Grandpa Simpson,* The Simpsons

scab (noun | /skæb/): A hated person; a wound that has crusted over

with dry patches of blood, the kind that five-year-olds pick at during storytime, causing their fellow classmates to recoil in disgust and alert the teacher, who promptly sends the child to the nurse because it's Friday afternoon and she does not have the energy to deal with bodily fluids.

Origin: If you're wondering, "Does this word have anything to do with the unspeakably repulsive skin condition, scabies? The one where mites burrow into the flesh, lay eggs, and induce uncontrollable itching fits?" Well, no, but it was a good guess. *Scab* hails from the Old English word *sceabb* ("itch") and the Old Norse *skabb* ("scab"). *Scabies*, in comparison, comes from the Latin *scabĕre* ("to scratch"). Some sources suggest both words have roots in the Proto-Indo-European prefix *(s)kep-* meaning "to scrape," which would make sense considering scabies makes you want to scrape your skin off.

> **❝** Did you ever notice how awful your face looks in a mirror in a restroom that has florescent lights? Every cut, scrape, scratch, scar, scab, bruise, boil, bump, pimple, zit, wart, welt, and abscess you've had since birth all seem to come back at the same time. And all you can think of is 'I gotta get the f— outta here!' **❞**

—*George Carlin,* George Carlin: Jammin' in New York

scalp

(verb / noun | /skælp/): The layer of skin covering the top of the head that is prone to afflictions like flaky dandruff, balding, and anger-inducing frizz; the act of tearing off another person's scalp and carrying it around like a trophy, similar to how cats carry around rat corpses because they think it is impressive.

Origin: Presumably Scandanavian, though no one can pin down the exact connection. Related to the Old Norse *skálpr* ("sheath") and *skalli* ("bald head"), the Danish *skalp* ("husk"), and the Middle Low German *schulpe* ("shell").

> 66 If my hair gets any frizzier, I'll shave it to the scalp. Or light it on fire. Whichever is easier. 99
>
> —*Victoria Scott,* Fire & Flood

schlub (noun | /ʃlʌb/): A person so worthless, the dictionary couldn't bother to give them a real name and settled on this garbled grunt instead.

schmear (verb / noun | /ʃmɪə/): As a noun: a small amount of a spreadable substance, a collective group of related things, or a bribe. As a verb: to spread or to flatter. As a sound: terrible, like the kind of word a nerdy high school biology teacher would utter during a lab experiment, letting globs of spit bubble up at the corner of his mouth as he says, "Now, kids, just take the sample and scccchhhhhmmmmear it onto the slide."

Origin: Sometimes written as *schmeer*, this term comes from the Yiddish term *shmirn* meaning "to smear" or "to flatter," which, honestly, is not much better.

> **What is a pap smear? Or is it 'schmear' like the cream cheese?**
>
> —*Michael Scott,*
> The Office

scrotum (noun | /ˈskroʊdəm/):

The external pouch that contains the testicles. *Scrotum* may be the most scientific way of talking about a man's family jewels, but that does not mean it is the best name for them. There are plenty of other slang words out there that do not induce nearly as much discomfort as scrotum. For example: *danglies*, *tweedledee and tweedledum*, *cojones*, *nuggets*, and *kangaroo apples*. See? Much better.

Origin: Taken directly from the Latin word of the same name, *scrotum*, which was likely inspired both by *scortum* ("a skin") and *scrautum* ("a hide bag used to carry arrows").

66 At the age of fourteen a Zoroastrian named Vilma ritualistically shaved my testicles. There really is nothing like a shorn scrotum... it's breathtaking. I highly suggest you try it. 99

—*Dr. Evil,* Austin Powers: International Man of Mystery

secrete (verb | /sɪˈkriːt/): To discharge or produce. Nothing good is ever secreted. For example: sweat, blood, oil, poison, bile, hormones. Do any of those make you feel warm and tingly inside? (Aside from, you know, the hormones and maybe the poison?)

Origin: From the Latin *sēcernĕre*, "to separate." Was also likely the back-formation of the noun secretion, which stems from the French *sécrétion* and the Latin *secretionem* meaning "a separation."

66 We've got nothing to do with the war. Maybe that's why we're on this ship, because we're not good enough to fight. Because our glands don't secrete enough adrenaline, or our great-great-grandmothers were afraid of the dark or something. 99

—*Doug Roberts,* Mister Roberts

seep **(verb | /sip/):** To ooze out, slowly, like clotted molasses trying to squeeze through a pinhole or blood escaping through a paper cut. You never hear someone say "joy seeped into her body" because good things don't seep—they explode. Bad things, on the other hand, inch along like a slug on concrete, because they know you are in a hurry and they do not mind making you wait.

Origin: Possibly a variant of the Old English word *sipian* meaning "to seep."

66 Dip the apple in the brew. Let the sleeping death seep through. There! On the skin! The symbol of what lies within. Now turn red to tempt Snow White, to make her hunger for a bite. 99

—*The Evil Queen,* Snow White and the Seven Dwarves

sinew **(noun | /ˈsɪnju/):** A piece of fibrous tissue connecting muscles to bones, none of which are particularly pleasant.

singleton **(noun | /ˈsɪŋg(ə)ltən/):** A cringeworthy nickname for single people that's still, somehow, not as bad as *spinster*.

slaw **(noun | /slɔ/):** Also known as coleslaw, slaw is a salad consisting of finely chopped cabbage mixed with a dressing like mayonnaise. Or, put plainly, goopy lettuce shavings. The word feels like saliva pooling in your mouth and dripping out of the corner.

Origin: A botched translation of the Dutch word *koolsla*, a combination of *kool* meaning "cabbage" and *sla* meaning "salad."

> ❝Nobody likes sweaty coleslaw.❞
>
> *—Aaron Sanchez*

sleet **(noun | /slit/):** A slushee that you can't drink. Seriously, what's the point?

Origin: This word for "partially thawed snow" probably comes from the Old English *slét* meaning "hail."

> ❝I'm better than you, Sleet.❞
>
> *—Snow*

slither

(**verb** | /ˈslɪðər/): To slide on the ground as a form of movement. When we describe something that "slithers," there is a zero percent chance that that something is cute and cuddly and has a spot atop the "animals that should have their own annual calendars" list. Why? Because anything that has to writhe its scaly, limbless body through dirt has no reason to be displayed in the office, the bedroom, or any place where adults or impressionable children might see it. Even saying the word *slither*, which causes the tongue to bump against the gap along the bottom teeth like an angry snake trying to escape, sends goosebumps down the spine.

Origin: From the very dated term *slidder* which means "to slip, to slide." (Yes, like the childhood toy.) Eventually, the *dd* turned into a *th*, giving us this slimy term.

> ❝ Death and disaster are at our shoulders every second of our lives, trying to get at us. Missing, a lot of the time. A lot of miles on the motorway without a front wheel blow-out. A lot of viruses that slither through our bodies without snagging. A lot of pianos that fall a minute after we've passed. Or a month, it makes no difference. So unless we're going to get down on our knees and give thanks every time disaster misses, it makes no sense to moan when it strikes. ❞

—*Hugh Laurie,* The Gun Seller

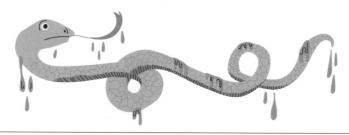

slubberdegullion (noun |

/ˌslʌbədɪˈɡʌljən/): You guessed it: a slobbering and/or slovenly person.

sludge (noun | /ˈslʌdʒ/): The slimy, earthy mud or slush that

oozes beneath your feet when you walk along a wet riverbank, the brown goop
burping as you squish the air bubbles out of its sopping clumpy form. Nothing
can make a literal wet mound of dirt sound or look good. Listen: Cotton Candy
Sludge. Kitten Sludge. Heated Blanket Sludge. Cuddle Sludge. Every iteration of
sludge makes you feel like you need a hot bath and if that is not an indicator of
grossness, what is?

Origin: It comes from the 1640s, but that is all we really know. Some believe the
word is a variant of *slush* ("watery result of melted snow and ice") or the Middle
English *slutch* ("mud").

66 The nuclear generator
of brain sludge is
television. 99

—*Dave Barry*

slug (verb | /sləg/):

The slow and slimy moth larvae that slinks from place to place, leaving a trail of sludge in its wake, with no regard for the human gag reflex and how people might react to its goopy body. As a noun, it can also mean a hefty lump, a lazy person, a gulp of liquor, a heavy blow, or a piece of metal. As a verb: to drink in gulps and to strike angrily. In every case, *slug* sounds like a mix of *slither* and *glug*, a combination that should frankly be illegal.

Origin: Of Scandinavian origin, likely related to the Swedish *slogga* ("to be slow or sluggish") and the Norwegian *slugg* ("a heavy body") and *sluggje* ("a heavy, slow person"). This "lazy person" or "lazy movement" definition was the first to appear along with "shell-less snail." Slug's metal definition appeared in the 1600s (probably inspired by a slug's resemblance to a tiny, deformed lead bullet) and was followed by the definition of *slug* as "a heavy blow," which may have been a variant of the word *slaughter*.

> **❝** It seems to me the worst of all the plagues is the slug, the snail without a shell. He is beyond description repulsive, a mass of sooty, shapeless slime, and he devours everything. **❞**
>
> —*Celia Thaxter,*
> An Island Garden

slurp

(verb / noun | /slərp/): To eat or drink something noisily; one who consumes something noisily, often to the dismay of neighboring dinner patrons who came to sip their soup and wine in peace.

> 66 If I hear you slurp your coffee one more time, I'm going to commit myself to a psych ward. 99
>
> —*Every person on the internet*

smarmy (adjective | /ˈsmɑrmi/): Marked by smugness or sleaziness. Ingratiating, but in an insincere way. Smarmy is the guy on Tinder who showers you with compliments in an attempt to get your number then, when you refuse, hits you with a string of unspeakable insults. Smarmy is the steely action star who chuckles at anyone who benches less than 200 pounds at the gym but then crumbles at the first sign of any real danger. Smarmy is the recent film school graduate who asks you about your favorite movie then snickers when you don't say the low-budget, art house Greta Gerwig film that they are thinking of. Smarmy is ugly.

Origin: From the colloquial word *smarm* meaning "to smear" or "to slick down." The phrase "to smear with flattery" became common around the 1900s and from there, this definition was born.

66 Keep the change, I don't need it as much as, well, some people. 99

—What a smarmy CEO says to a barista as he hands over a $100 bill and pointedly stares at her tattered jeans

I.M. PERFECTION

smear (verb / noun | /smɪ(ə)r/): Cousin of *schmear*, smear means to coat something with a sticky substance, to defame someone through insulting or slanderous comments, or (as a noun) a material spread thinly.

snot (noun | /snɑt/): A piece of mucus and/or a stuck-up person. Snot is the sound you hear when your nose is filled with snot and you attempt to breathe in. Try it.

Origin: From the Old English *gesnot* and Middle English *snotte* meaning "nasal mucus," this word originally meant "the snuff of a candle" back in the 1400s. Did someone see the drippy, half-hardened wax dripping down the side of a candle one day and say, "Hey, that sort of looks like the stuff that comes out of my nose, maybe we should call it the same thing"? Possibly, but no dictionary will admit it.

❝ God wiped snot out of his nose and that was you. ❞

—*Stephen King,* The Shining

soggy **(adjective | /ˈsɑgi/):** Overly moist, which is not pleasant in any context. Soggy cereal. Soggy dog. Soggy bread. See?

soil **(verb / noun | /sɔɪl/):** As a noun, the surface of the earth or dirt. As a verb, to ruin or to tarnish. It can also refer to the act of peeing oneself, aka, what your Sims do whenever you take away their free will to satisfy your own sick God complex.

spatchcock **(noun | /ˈspætʃˌkɑk/):** A form of preparing meat that involves removing the creature's backbone, splitting it open, and plucking off any remaining feathers or fur.

spine **(noun | /spaɪn/):** A string of vertebrae stretching from the neck to the small of the back. Present in most humans, with the exception of Twitter trolls, heartless bosses, and roommates who passive aggressively remove your things from the living room when you are not home because it doesn't match the Pinterest aesthetic that they are so desperately trying to curate.

spit (verb / noun | /spɪt/): What happens when you look at a delicious piece of food and feel a hot, watery substance oozing out of the glands in your mouth? Spit happens. Spit is the bubbly, sticky goo that swirls around in the dark, dank cavern between your lips, pooling beneath your tongue until you decide to swallow it or launch it off the side of a building onto the head of an unlucky passing stranger. It is only good for one of two things: breaking up food particles or tormenting your younger siblings by holding them down and letting a long, stringy spit particle dangle above their face.

Origin: From the Old English *spittan* ("to expel saliva") and the German *spitzen* ("of imitative origin") and weirdly, *not* from the Latin word *spūtum*, literally meaning "spit" (see: **sputum**). Spit is like spittle ("a tiny glob of spit") except more grown up. Like, spit probably does its own taxes and drinks its coffee black.

SPIT
happens

10-40

❝ The first kiss I had was the most disgusting thing in my life. The girl injected about a pound of saliva into my mouth, and when I walked away I had to spit it all out. ❞

—*Leonardo DiCaprio*

spittle (noun | /ˈspɪt(ə)l/): A baby spit, the kind that likes to jump onto people's faces without asking and lounge on the corner of your mouth just waiting to stir up trouble.

spittoon (noun | /spɪˈtun/): A receptacle for spit. Warm, white, gooey, looks-like-a-clump-of-spider-eggs spit.

splog (noun | /splag/): A spam blog. Which is to say, a blog designed to look real but is actually just a series of sponsored links or ads paid for by outside sites that are determined to sell you "face-enhancing lotion" or "magic beanstalk seeds" or the like.

spork (noun | /spɔːk/): A fork with a soft spot. A spoon with too much edge. A utensil with an identity crisis.

sputum

(noun | /ˈspjudəm/): You know in medical shows when the charming-yet-brilliant doctor declares that they have solved the case, only to turn around and find the patient hacking up an unknown brown-yellow liquid that looks like undercooked scrambled eggs? That is sputum. And, like its name suggests, it often "spews" out of a person's mouth when they are sick, shooting speckles of mucus, blood, pus, and bacteria through the air like the world's worst Pollock painting.

Origin: This one actually comes from the Latin word *spūtum*, meaning "spit."

66 The Bible is a sanctum; the world, sputum. 99

—*Franz Kafka*

squelch (noun | /skwɛltʃ/): The noise produced by a soft, weak body hitting the ground. Nothing says "humans are just glorified bags of water and blood held together by skin" more than a loud sloshy squelch.

squirt (verb / noun | /skwərt/): To shoot liquid out of a small opening; to spurt; and, brace yourself, to expel excrement in a thin stream. In noun form: the result of such expulsion; an endearing title you give to someone much smaller than you, probably while ruffling their hair and slipping them a few quarters so they can buy a raspberry sucker at the candy store. Also, one-half of the best aquatic Pokémon, Squirtle, who is much cuter than the word squirt would suggest.

Origin: From Middle English *squirten*. Cognate to Low German *swirtjen*, meaning "to squirt." Noun from the late Middle English *sqwyrt*, "diarrhea."

> ❝ This is unexpected...like squirt from aggressive grapefruit. ❞
>
> —*Earl Derr Biggers*

squish

(verb / noun | /skwɪʃ/): The noise you hear when you are walking to school on an abnormally sunny day in winter and your boots step into a puddle of not-quite-snow, not-quite-water. The cry a moist towel makes when you wring it in your hands post-dishes. The soft squelching sound your baby's diaper lets out when there's one too many poops inside. No matter where the squish comes from, you know it is going to be damp, smelly, and probably a little uncomfortable.

Origin: Imitative etymology, meaning someone out there heard a squishing sound for the first time and went: "Yeah, let's just call it that."

> **"** Three tomatoes are walking down the street—a papa tomato, a mama tomato, and a little baby tomato. Baby tomato starts lagging behind. Papa tomato gets angry, goes over to the baby tomato, and squishes him...and says, 'ketchup.' **"**
>
> —*Mia Wallace,* Pulp Fiction

taint

taint (verb | /teɪnt/): To contaminate, physically or morally. Things that taint: paint (if you pour it into drinking water), blood (if you are in a sterile hospital room), Harry Potter novels (if you are one of *those* parents), cooties (if you are under the age of nine), and bacteria (if you are a slab of meat).

Origin: From Middle English *teynten* meaning "to convict" and the Old French *ataindre* meaning "to seize." This definition lent itself to the contemporary "contaminate" use around the 1600s.

> **❝** There is no odor so bad as that which arises from goodness tainted. **❞**

—*Henry David Thoreau*, Walden

tentacle (noun | /ˈtɛntək(ə)l/): There are two reasons that

humans do not have tentacles. One, evolution. Two, because waking up and seeing eight tentacles in the mirror every morning would surely kill us faster than any illness or murderer could. If octopi are the spiders of the sea, then tentacles are the ocean's slimy, spindly bug leg equivalent and they should stay deep beneath the surface—far, far away from humans.

Origin: Apparently, from the Latin word *tentāculum* meaning "a feeler," which should by all rights be what we call our fingers: "You may now place the ring on your new wife's feeler."

> ❝ It's better to be an octopus than a fish. If an octopus loses a tentacle to a predator, the octopus will survive with seven tentacles left for itself. ❞
>
> —*Gene Simmons*

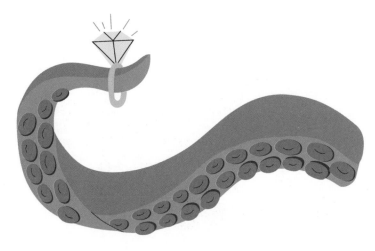

thusly (adverb | /ˈðəsli/): A pretentious variation of "thus" that only condescending college students and Ross Gellar say.

toad (noun | /toʊd/): In the beginning, God created the heavens and the earth. And then God said, "Let there be light," and there was light. And then God said, "Let there be frogs!" and there were frogs. And then God said, "Let there be something almost identical to frogs but just a little uglier!" and there were toads.

treacle (noun | /ˈtriːk(ə)l/): In a literal sense, unrefined sugar like molasses. In a broader sense, sentimentality so sweet that it's sickening.

trenchant (adjective | /ˈtrɛn(t)ʃənt/): If someone is speaking to you in a *trenchant* (read: incisive and sharp) tone of voice, it is because they want to yell at you but, for some reason, can't, forcing them to mumble vaguely disparaging jabs at you through clenched teeth instead.

turgid (adjective | /ˈtərdʒəd/): An adjective meaning swollen or inflated. Probably the name of the least popular dwarf in the fantasy book your brother is reading.

über (prefix | /'ubər/): Prefix denoting supremacy and a subpar car service run by the rich egomaniac you hated in college.

udder (noun | /'ədər/): Cow nipples.

ugly (adjective | /'əgli/): Unattractive. Grotesque. Ill-shaped. Loathsome. Offensive. Appalling. Repulsive. Foul. Tainted. Corrupt. Disagreeable. Vile. Nasty. Gross. And the very crux of this entire book. If you do not understand what it means at this point, you are on your own.

Origin: Fittingly taken from the Old Norse term *uggligr* meaning "to be feared or dreaded." Thankfully, this bold definition has since been toned down.

66 Beauty is only skin deep, but ugly goes clean to the bone. 99

—*Dorothy Parker*

unctuous (adjective | /ˈʌŋktjuːəs/): This adjective means
"having the oily or greasy qualities of an unguent" and makes the speaker
immediately feel like they have a frog stuck in their throat.

Uranus (noun | /ˈjʊərənəs/): The seventh planet in our solar
system that every junior high astronomy teacher dreads mentioning, in fear of
triggering a giggle storm.

urchin (noun | /ˈɜrtʃən/): A shortened name for "sea-urchin" or a
not-so-nice way to refer to your friend's mischievous kid.

urp (noun | /ərp/): The sound of a belch or one of those dry gags that you
cough into the toilet when your body decides it needs to vomit even though you
haven't eaten anything in seven hours.

uvula (noun | /ˈjuːvjʊlə/): The eyedrop-shaped piece of flesh that dangles in the back of the throat just waiting for something to lightly poke it so that it can induce a stream of projectile vomit so embarrassing, you will vow to never leave the house again.

Origin: Get ready. This word comes from the Latin *ūvula* meaning "little grape," making this the cutest definition on this ugly list. And, boys, for the record: this has *nothing* to do with the urethra.

> **"Hit 'em in the uvula!"**
>
> —*Ron Burgundy*

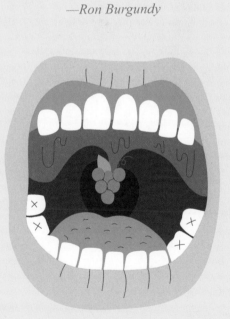

vascular (adjective | /ˈvaskjʊlə/): Having the form of vessels.
Just as gross (if not grosser) than the word *artery*. (For proof, see: **artery**.)

vein (noun | /veɪn/): A small vessel that carries blood from the
capillaries to the heart; a distinctive quality or style; a water channel in a rock.
Veins are nothing more than bloody spiderwebs stretching through the body,
ready to spring a leak at the first sign of something pointy. Maybe it is the *v* or
maybe it is the resemblance to the villain Bane, but either way, this word clogs
my heart and kills all joy.

Origin: Drawn from the Middle English *veyne* ("vein"), Old French *veine*
("artery"), and the Latin *vena* ("blood vessel"). The "channel" and "style"
definitions of this word did not spring up until the twelfth and thirteenth century.

66 If I close my eyes and think
of Hollywood, all I see is one
big varicose vein. **99**

—*Marilyn Monroe*

ventricle (noun | /ˈvɛntrɪk(ə)l/): Cavities in the heart
through which blood circulates. Why is this gross? Picture a bunch of vents with blood trickling through them, like some deleted scene from *The Shining*, and you should figure it out pretty quickly.

vermin (noun | /ˈvərmən/): Destructive or devious plants,
animals, or humans. Must be said in a seething tone.

vile (adjective | /vaɪl/): Morally despicable or depraved. No relation to
Nick Viall of *Bachelor* fame and beauty.

VIP (noun | /viː aɪ ˈpiː/): An acronym for "Very Important Person."
The original version of this phrase, APWBTAIETHAASTTAI ("A Person Who Believes They Are Important Enough To Have An Acronym Stating That They Are Important"), didn't quite roll off the tongue and had to be shortened.

viscous (adjective | /ˈvɪskəs/): What is seven letters long and sounds like a snake deflating? *Viscous*, an adjective meaning "having a gluey consistency." Anything that is thick and moves like a slug taking its precious time can be considered viscous. Yes, that includes your dad.

Origin: Taken directly from the Latin *viscōsus* meaning "sticky" (makes sense) and *viscum* meaning "birdlime made from mistletoe" (makes less sense).

> ❝ When I was ten years old, I saw a big, fat beetle get squished. I don't recall the circumstances, but that's not important. It's the result that stuck with me. The beetle's thick, viscous insides so closely resembled a crushed blueberry that, to this day, I can't eat raw blueberries without feeling nauseous. ❞
>
> —*Jeremy Robinson*

warmonger (noun | /ˈwɔrˌmaŋɡər/): Someone who advocates aggression with other countries. Make love, not warmongers, people.

---

wart (noun | /ˈwɔ(ə)rt/): A hard protuberance on the skin with an extraordinary ability to scare away small children, no matter how many times you tell them that it is benign bump and not at all cootie-related. On the scale of gross skin ailments, it falls between a skin tag and a swollen pimple.

Origin: This word stems primarily from the Old English *wearte* ("wart"), though it also has connections to the Old Frisian *warte*, Old Saxon *warte*, Dutch *wrat*, Old High German *warza*, and the Old Norse *varta*.

❝❝ I desire you would use all your skill to paint my picture truly like me, and not flatter me at all; but remark all these roughnesses, pimples, warts and everything as you see me, otherwise I will never pay a farthing for it. ❞❞

—*Oliver Cromwell,* bravely instructing painter Sir Peter Lely to incorporate each and every blemish into his official portrait (which ultimately led to the phrase "warts and all")

wean (verb | /wiːn/): This word, meaning "to gradually detach from a habit or item," originally meant "to force a child to try food other than their mother's milk."

weasel (verb / noun | /ˈwiːz(ə)l/): A small bloodthirsty animal, a person that behaves like a small bloodthirsty animal, or a person that behaves like a small bloodthirsty animal behaving like a small bloodthirsty animal.

Weimaraner (noun | /ˈwaɪməˌrɑnər/): A hunting dog with a name that sounds like a German torture device.

welt (noun | /wɛlt/): A swollen mark that forms at the site of a hard blow and is painful to touch and painful to look at.

wharf (noun | /hwɔːf/): A wooden structure built along the shore where boats may dock. What a whale's bark might sound like.

wifey

(noun | /ˈwaɪfi/): A term of endearment so sickly sweet, it results in 13 percent of divorces every year. (A false statistic, but it could be true.)

Origin: Probably coined by the same cretin who invented hubby. (See: *hubby*.)

❝I'm cut from a different cloth, baby. It's called 'wifey' material.❞

—*A very real poster you can buy at a very real T-shirt shop*

worm

(noun | /wərm/): Any type of burrowing, elongated invertebrate with a soft, limbless body. (Is that a description of a real creature or a monster from a nightmare video game? Hard to say.) These slimy, eyeless animals use their pointy, slimy nubbin heads to push through dirt until they inevitably crawl into the hands of some curious toddler who will tear them apart with pine needles and leave their bodies baking in the sun. Unpopular opinion? *Good riddance.*

Origin: A variant of the Old English *wyrm* meaning "serpent," "snake," or "dragon." Yes, those wriggling noodles you find in the sandbox were named after winged, fire-breathing lizards. Talk about an origin story.

> **❝** The early bird gets the worm. The early worm...gets eaten. **❞**
>
> —*Norman Ralph Augustine*

wound (verb / noun | /wund/): To inflict a blow to someone's body or pride, possibly through violence or harsh words about their really stylish and practical fanny pack.

wrinkly (adjective | /ˈrɪŋk(ə)li/): Full of lines or wrinkles. Characteristic of unironed laundry, pruny fingers, hairless cats, E.T. the Extra Terrestrial, and old people. It is most likely the thing your mother is pointing to in the mirror when she says, "Look, I'm old now! You've made me old!"

Origin: A back-formation of *wrinkled*, which was ripped from the stem of Old English *gewrinclod* meaning "wrinkled" or "crooked."

> **❝** She was so small and wrinkly as an infant. She looked like a baked potato that was microwaved too long. **❞**
>
> —*Doug Gardner,* Atypical

x-ray (verb / noun | /ˈɛksˌreɪ/): The digital images produced when electromagnetic rays are beamed through the body, usually to reveal the internal composition of something; the act of examining a patient using these rays; the type of vision hormone-charged twelfth graders wish they had so they could check out their crush-of-the-week more efficiently.

xerox (verb | /ˈzɪˌrɑks/): To make a copy. A term only used by dull professionals or preteen boys determined to scan their behinds from every conceivable angle on a xerographic machine. And nothing says "gross" more than 149 pages of smushed, hairless buttcrack photos.

Origin: In 1938, Chester Carlson, an attorney and physicist, invented the world's first elementary "photocopy" using a photoconductor and toner. Eight years later, Joseph Wilson, president of the Haloid Photographic Company, took Carlson's invention and ran with it, developing the device into what we know today as a xerox machine. The company coined a new term for the process, xenography (meaning "dry writing"), by combining the Greek roots *xeros* ("dry") and *-ography* (after photography).

> **“**All I did my first year at *Vogue* was xerox.**”**
>
> —*Vera Wang*

yolk (noun | /jouk/): Literally: the yellow center of an egg.

Figuratively: the innermost part of something. While some people find the snotty texture of yolks repulsive, others take issue with the pronunciation itself. Say the word *yolk* out loud. Notice how your throat twitches in confusion and anger when it has to pull the *olk* sound out of its depths? This word was not made to be liked.

Origin: Formerly spelled *yelk*, *yolk* is believed to have originated with the Old English word *geoloca*, an etymology that makes more sense when you realize that the prefix *ge-* during this time could be pronounced *yee*. Going back further, *geoloca* comes from *geolu*, meaning "yellow." Over time, this word evolved into its current form, likely as a result of people trying to shorten the word *yellow*.

❝ I'm frightened of eggs, worse than frightened, they revolt me. That white round thing without any holes…have you ever seen anything more revolting than an egg yolk breaking and spilling its yellow liquid? Blood is jolly, red. But egg yolk is yellow, revolting. ❞

—*Alfred Hitchcock*

za (noun | /zɑː/): The worst possible nickname for pizza.

zit (noun | /zɪt/): A bulging, swollen, throbbing, pus-filled, eye-catching, tear-inducing, oh-my-god-everyone's-definitely-staring-at-it, kill-me-now pimple.

Origin: Related to the English *chit* ("wart") and the German *zitze* ("teat").

> **"**It's difficult to have everybody like everything you do. I don't know anybody that's perfect and doesn't have a zit somewhere.**"**
>
> —*Gordon Bethune*

zygote (noun | /ˈzaɪˌɡoʊt/): When a mommy and daddy make love, their gametes merge together to create a zygote, a eukaryotic cell containing all of the genetic information required to make a living, breathing, pooping human. What could be grosser than that?

Acknowledgments

The opportunity to write *The Illustrated Compendium of Ugly English Words* literally fell from the internet void into my lap. For that, I need to thank my wonderful publisher John Whalen without whom none of this would be possible, my delightful editor Margaret McGuire Novak who endured my endless string of silly questions with total and utter grace, our fabulous proofreader Rebekah Slonim, our designer Melissa Gerber who found a way to make all of this ugly content look beautiful, and our talented illustrator Rebecca Pry for helping to create a project so nauseating that it has already caused at least seven people to vomit, probably.

I would also like to thank my parents for supporting my decision to major in English all those years ago, my brother and step siblings for their constant support and occasional heckles, my Nana and Uckie for making a place thousands of miles away from Boston feel like home, and all 5,372 members of the Vendetti family for, well, everything else. I am grateful for my friends, who humored all of my strange word-related requests for months and, for some reason, still don't hate me for it: Araz Havan, Linnéa Ryan, Danielle Peters, Saraf Rahman, Alison Matte, Amanda Douglas, Nina Umpierrez, Polly Bickford-Duane, Charlotte Fressilli, Emily Bryer, Daniela Alves, Drew Alemania, Isabelle Carasso, Augusta Harris, Nicole Ramberg, Lauren Arnold, Stephen Carrier, and last but not least, Sophie "Woman With Light Skin Tone Dancing" Lamzik.

There are also a few invaluable resources that deserve some credit: the *Oxford English Dictionary*, which taught me everything I never knew about the words I've always hated, HelloGiggles, which gave me a platform to explore my love for writing before I even knew it existed, and Twitter which provided me with a slew of strangers who were more than happy to flood my timeline with words that make them queasy.

I love you all.

About the Author

Born and raised in a small Massachusetts town that you've probably never heard of, Tyler Vendetti is a writer, reader, and dessert enthusiast with a relentless love for the English language. As a contributor to xoJane, TIME Online, *Cosmopolitan* magazine, HelloGiggles, The Penny Hoarder, Thought Catalog, and more, she has been dubbed the internet's resident "word queen" by her mom and at least one stranger on Twitter. Tyler has worked at NBCUniversal and is now a Writers' PA for Warner Bros. Entertainment, where she spends her days fetching coffee, reading scripts, and researching obscure ways to kill off your favorite characters. She is an out and proud nerd with a passion for comedy, horror movies, and restaurants that keep Christmas lights up year-round. You can find her on Twitter at @HeyThereFuture or at her apartment in Los Angeles, where she currently resides with her roommate and her invisible cat, Catsper.

About the Illustrator

Rebecca Pry is an illustrator and designer living in Warwick, New York. She received a BFA in illustration from Rhode Island School of Design in 2013. Rebecca's art adds a humorous twist to everyday items and scenes, and she has created patterns and graphics for home goods, books, accessories, and apparel. She regularly shows her work in local galleries in the Hudson Valley. When she is not drawing, she is outside in a brightly colored sweater. See more at rebeccapry.com.

PUBLISHING PRACTICAL & CREATIVE NONFICTION

Whalen Book Works is a small, independent book publishing company
based in Maine that combines top-notch design, unique formats,
and fresh content to create truly innovative gift books.

Our unconventional approach to bookmaking is a close-knit, creative, and
collaborative process among authors, artists, designers, editors, and
booksellers. We publish a small, carefully curated list each season, and
we take the time to make each book exactly what it needs to be.

We believe in giving back. That's why we plant one tree for every ten books
we print. Your purchase supports a tree in the Rocky Mountain National Park.

Get in touch!

Visit us at **Whalenbooks.com**
or write to us at
68 North Street, Kennebunkport, ME 04046

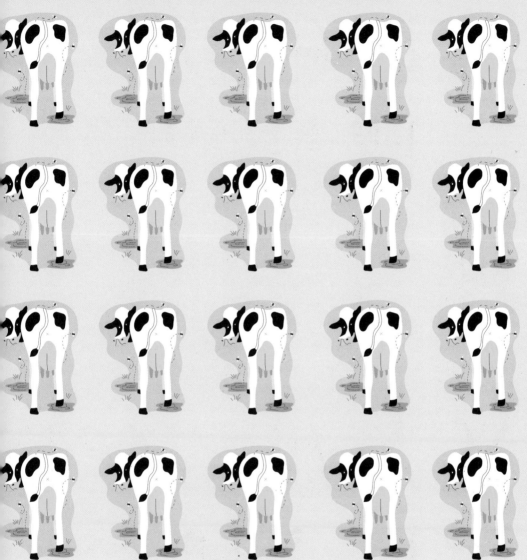